TJ

*Letts* EXPLORE

# Othello

WILLIAM SHAKESPEARE

D1434436

## Guide written by
## Stewart Martin

A *Letts* Literature

Every effort has been made to trace copyright holders and to obtain their permission for the use of copyright material. The author and publishers will gladly receive information enabling them to rectify any reference or credit in subsequent editions.

First published 1995
Reprinted 1997

Letts Educational
Aldine House
Aldine Place
London W12 8AW
Tel: 0181-740 2266

Text © Stewart Martin 1995

**Typeset by** Jordan Publishing Design

**Text design** Jonathan Barnard

**Cover and text illustrations** Hugh Marshall

**Graphic illustration** Hugh Marshall

Design © BPP (Letts Educational) Ltd

**British Library Cataloguing in Publication Data**
A CIP record for this book is available from the British Library

ISBN 1 85758 270 5

Printed and bound in Great Britain
by Ashford Colour Press Ltd,
Gosport, Hants.

Letts Educational is the trading name of BPP (Letts Educational) Ltd

# ■ Contents

# ■ Plot synopsis

Othello is a Moorish General serving the authorities in Venice. He has secretly eloped with and married the much younger Desdemona, the beautiful Caucasian daughter of a Venetian Senator. Othello is a highly respected and influential military leader and a loving and devoted husband, but is isolated from the social world into which he has married. He is sent to lead the defence of Cyprus, which the Venetians fear is about to be attacked by the Turks. Othello's trusted aide, Iago, goes with him. He says he has many reasons for hating Othello and plots to destroy him. Iago dupes Roderigo, a Venetian gentleman who loves Desdemona and pays Iago to help him. Othello is persuaded by Iago that his wife is committing adultery with Cassio, his Captain. He is convinced of this in part by a trick which Iago engineers, using a handkerchief which Othello gave to Desdemona and which Iago persuades his own wife, Emilia, to steal for him to use. Othello's lack of trust is used by Iago to inflame his insane jealousy to the point where he murders Desdemona by smothering her in her bed. Emilia is instrumental in exposing the evil manipulations of her husband and convincing Othello that his wife was innocent. When he learns of his terrible mistake, Othello kills himself.

*Note:* Different editions of a Shakespeare play are usually very similar, although they may show occasional variations in spelling, punctuation and the arrangement of the lines. You may even come across differences in act or scene divisions, but this should produce no difficulties for you in identifying the particular point or section being commented on in this Guide. The quotations and comments in this Guide are referenced to the Arden edition of the play.

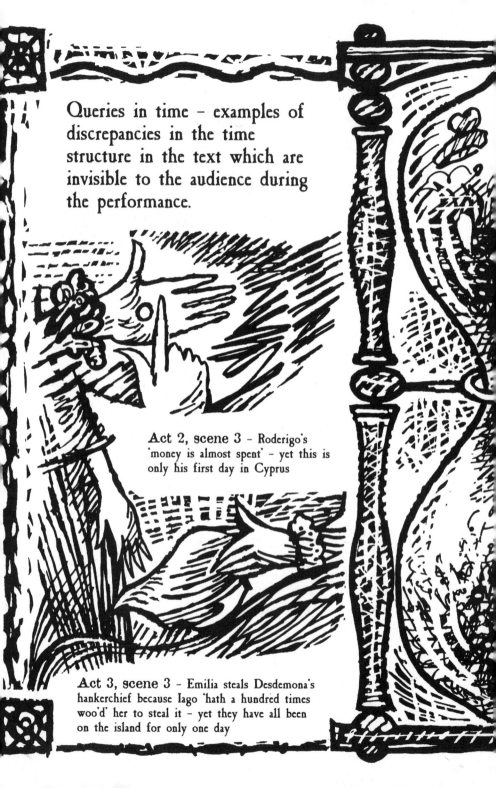

Queries in time – examples of discrepancies in the time structure in the text which are invisible to the audience during the performance.

Act 2, scene 3 – Roderigo's 'money is almost spent' – yet this is only his first day in Cyprus

Act 3, scene 3 – Emilia steals Desdemona's hankerchief because Iago 'hath a hundred times woo'd' her to steal it – yet they have all been on the island for only one day

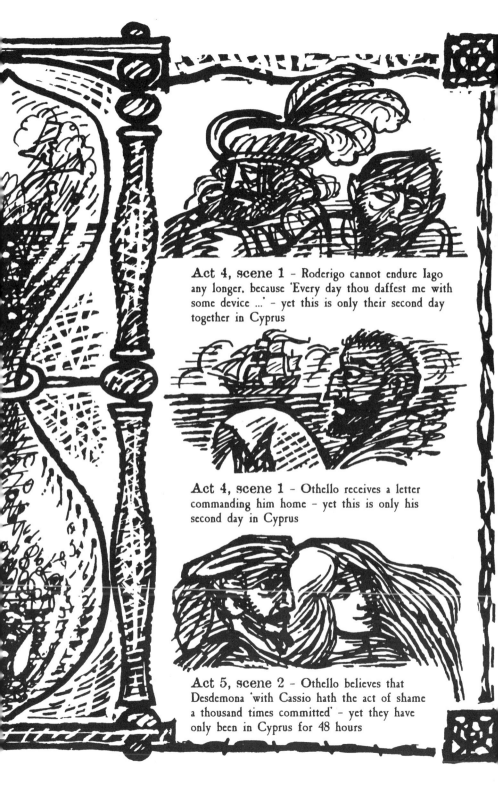

**Act 4, scene 1** – Roderigo cannot endure Iago any longer, because 'Every day thou daffest me with some device ...' – yet this is only their second day together in Cyprus

**Act 4, scene 1** – Othello receives a letter commanding him home – yet this is only his second day in Cyprus

**Act 5, scene 2** – Othello believes that Desdemona 'with Cassio hath the act of shame a thousand times committed' – yet they have only been in Cyprus for 48 hours

# ■ Who's who in *Othello*

Othello

## Othello

As the first significant black character in English literature, Othello's Moorish complexion (clearly intended to be black African) would have had an immediate impact on Elizabethan audiences. Shakespeare knew that many of them would be very prejudiced and would have associated a Moor with brutality, ignorance, evil and sexual immorality. The character of Othello both confirmed and contradicted these contemporary expectations in a number of significant ways. Although black – and therefore attracting the audience's traditional Elizabethan suspicion of Moors – Othello is in fact sympathetically drawn. It is the scheming, malevolent Iago who appears as an honest and trustworthy servant, but who is in reality the depiction of evil incarnate. It is Othello who is the highly promoted and respected General at the start of the play, at first a man of calm integrity, a dutiful and loving husband to the younger, white Desdemona and a pillar of Venetian society. Central to the tragic action of the play is the transformation of this noble character, in front of our eyes, into an irrational murderer under the evil influence of the jealous Iago. Also central is what many have seen as Othello's almost passive role in the action of the play – simply a reactor to events – which sometimes makes it difficult to see him in the traditional mould of the Shakespearean tragic hero; someone like Hamlet, for example, who understands and accepts his tragic fate.

It is also possible to see the character of Othello from extremes: as the noble, heroic, loving innocent trapped and destroyed by the malign Iago, *or* as the self-admiring, vicious, weak, cruel and arrogant upstart who loves no one as much as himself and who fully deserves his comeuppance. You may find something useful in each of these views, but you should carefully weigh all the evidence yourself. By the time we first meet Othello (in Act 1, scene 2) we have had a considerable amount of information about him from others, mostly unflattering. We have been told that 'the

Moor', who is also called 'the thick lips', is proud and bombastic and is an 'old black ram' and 'the devil'. Although these views come from Iago and Roderigo, both of whom have cause to resent Othello, they create a strong negative impression in the mind of the audience. On the other hand, the Duke of Venice clearly thinks a great deal of Othello as a General and leader of others, entrusting him with the defence of Cyprus. The previous governor, Montano, is also an early admirer of this 'full soldier'.

Our own first impressions of Othello are affected by his dignified manner, his charismatic presence, his exotic background and his wide experience of the world as seen through Elizabethan eyes. But we should note that, like Macbeth, Othello's experience of the world is largely military; both characters find themselves unable to deal with the subterfuges and politics which exist outside the military sphere.

As Iago's work on Othello begins to ˚stoke up the furnace of jealousy and his sense of wronged honour, we see a change in Othello's behaviour. Even after the murder of Desdemona, however, we can appreciate the sincerity of character which allows him to accept full responsibility for what he has done and then to deliberately take his own life in self-punishment. However, we might review our initial impressions of Othello as we witness his later actions and be more aware of the possibility that it is his pride which is his ultimate undoing, not his innocence or Iago's malevolence. From this perspective it is easier to see Othello as the traditional Shakesperian tragic hero; an almost perfect character who, through one fatal mistake, finds himself in circumstances which propel him from the height of fortune and regard to complete destruction, and through which he achieves part redemption.

## Desdemona

The character of Desdemona (the name means 'unhappy' or 'evil fate') is the most consistent in the play. She does not change, symbolising the values of helpless good and wronged innocence throughout. Although she is spoken of as a girl and is at first thought even by her own father to have innocently fallen prey to Othello's lust and charms, when we first meet her she seems a mature, confident and perceptive woman who is fully aware of her own feelings and is deeply in love with her husband. However, some people find Desdemona's goodness to be rather overdone – somewhat too good to be true – and you should consider the extent to which this seems a fair criticism to you. Iago's perception of Venetian women is certainly very different, as we see in his conversations with Roderigo and Othello, where Iago suggests that they are unfaithful and corrupt and that Desdemona is worse than a common prostitute. Iago's wife, Emilia, shares her husband's sordid view of the world, as we see from her conversation with Desdemona in Act 2. Desdemona's character is less central than that of Othello or Iago and so it is appropriate that it is less developed, for the role she plays and the things she represents are in some ways more important than her character. Her relationship with other characters is, as her name implies, the most important part of her, although she is a credible person in her own right in the play, not a two-dimensional caricature. She is mature and balanced in her views: she sees a divided duty between her father and her husband at the start of the play; she is sympathetic to the situation of others, like Cassio. She is concerned for Othello when he feels unwell and for his safety when his ship is delayed; she expresses an interest in the opinions of others, like Emilia, but is tactful when they are different to hers.

Desdemona is portrayed as vulnerable but pure. Her purity has been the subject of some dispute, usually revolving around the point (in Act 2, scene 1) where she exchanges bawdy comments with Iago and where, some say, a coarser side to her character emerges – one more in keeping with Iago's perceptions about all Venetian women. You should consider whether this compromises the view of Desdemona as a pure and innocent woman, or whether it simply shows us that she is not ignorant of the ways of the world and has made a conscious choice not to be corrupt. If the latter, you may conclude that Desdemona is merely showing in this scene that she is well able to deal with the banter and bawdy flirtations which would be commonplace in the social circles in which a wealthy young woman of those times would move. Her commitment to her husband is not merely spiritual, and embraces the physical and sexual aspects of a loving relationship – something upon which Othello's eventual jealousy and Iago's manipulation of it depend. Iago could not have succeeded at all if we (and

Othello) had seen Desdemona as a passionless woman devoid of all sexuality. When she lies about the loss of the handkerchief which her husband gave her, it is clear from the context that she does so out of concern not to upset Othello further, not because she wishes to deceive him or conceal some wrongdoing. Even in her dying words she blames herself for what has happened, not her foolish and jealous husband.

## Iago

Iago

Like Desdemona, the character of Iago represents certain values and attitudes towards the world and he does not develop or change throughout the play. He is named after the patron saint of Spain, England's great enemy at the time of the play's writing. Iago represents the opposite of everything Desdemona stands for, and the conflict between these two sets of values is a central feature of the play. Desdemona wishes for happiness, peace, reconciliation, order and love, because these are the things which give her life meaning. Iago wishes for death, destruction and anarchy. It is not that Iago does not believe in the things which Desdemona represents, but he feels that life has wrongly denied him these things and so he wishes to destroy them in others. Iago also feels that he has been passed over for promotion and that Cassio has been given the position which should have been his. Iago also suspects his own wife, Emilia, of having an adulterous affair with Othello and her comments to Desdemona in Act 4, scene 3 lend at least the possibility of weight to this suspicion. Furthermore, Iago feels belittled – almost criticised by implication – by the good qualities of others: he cannot endure the 'constant, noble, loving nature' of Othello; and he says that Cassio's 'daily beauty in his life… makes me ugly'.

Iago's feelings are driven by a passion of such intense strength that, even though we might understand his motives, it is difficult to feel that anything other than pure evil could compel him to such extremes of behaviour as a result. Iago also seems to take a powerful, sadistic delight in the damage which he causes. His effectiveness as a character in the play rests upon the way he is seen differently by the other characters, who see loyalty, honesty and trustworthiness, and by the audience, who watch a malevolent – almost satanic – character mercilessly manipulate others with the intention of completely destroying them. Hence Iago's open comment, 'I am not what I am'.

Iago is not simply a cipher, some kind of symbolic representation of evil, but is much more. He manipulates the perceptions of other characters with great skill, using lies which contain sufficient truth for us to see why it could be that anyone should believe them. Although Iago's suspicion of his wife's adultery is no more than that, he says that 'for mere suspicion of that kind' he will act as though it were certain. Iago falls prey to the same suspicion he generates in Othello and, through controlling the plot for most of the play, moves Othello towards his cynical view of the world.

However, Iago can only achieve his ends through the weakness of others. In this respect *Othello* is similar to the traditional Morality Play of the period, in which a character must choose between the devil (evil) and an angel (good). In choosing between Desdemona and Iago, it is Othello's inability to accept his own potential for love and trust which destroys him. At the end, only Iago's silence is left. Although Iago has offered the audience motives for his behaviour, it is difficult to relate the wrongs he supposes have been inflicted upon him with the amount of damage he tries to cause in recompense. Ironically, it is Iago's professed knowledge of human nature which lets him down at the crucial moment, for he has failed to allow for the nobler impulses of others and it is his own wife who turns against him.

## Roderigo

Roderigo

Roderigo, who loves Desdemona, pays Iago to help him in his attempts to win her affections, even though he knows she is married. Iago dupes this gullible Venetian gentleman to the extent that he becomes persuaded to attempt the murder of Cassio one dark night in Cyprus. (He has followed Desdemona there because he thinks Iago is close to securing her love for him.) Roderigo's foolishness in believing Iago anticipates the way Othello is similarly taken in by Iago's lies and insinuations, and his dramatic role at the start of the play allows the audience to gain an insight into Iago's scheming. The appearance of Roderigo is used at several points in the play in a similar way, when his conversations with Iago are usually accompanied by a soliloquy from the latter, who reveals to the audience even more of his deceptions. The character of Roderigo is not strongly drawn, but we see enough to know that he is a weak and pliant person who, although not without feeling and some moral conscience, is completely within the power of his malign employee. Roderigo would be happy to win Desdemona by any means and, like Othello, becomes entangled in Iago's scheming until it is impossible for him to escape. When Roderigo has some doubts about his venture and suggests that he may abandon seeking the affections of Desdemona, Iago decides, in a coldly calculating way, that he must be killed in case the truth about what Iago has really been up to is exposed.

## Cassio

Cassio

As the play opens, Othello has appointed Cassio as his Lieutenant. Iago feels this post should have gone to him and says that Cassio has no experience in warfare and so does not deserve the post. At the start of the play Cassio and Iago meet and we see how Cassio can neither understand nor share Iago's cynical and bitter views, especially about the marriage of Othello and Desdemona. Iago uses the courteous behaviour of Cassio as something which can be misinterpreted as lust, and turns this to account when persuading Othello to see his behaviour in this particular way. (Iago calls this 'ocular proof' of Desdemona's infidelity with Cassio.) Iago gets Cassio drunk and when he becomes involved in a brawl, Othello sacks him. When Cassio seeks Desdemona's help in pleading his case with Othello, Iago also uses this against him as further evidence of an illicit relationship between them. Iago's feelings against Cassio are further fuelled by jealousy, for Cassio is a handsome, educated and popular young man whom Iago also sees as 'almost damned in a fair wife' and with 'a daily beauty in his life'. As a Florentine, Cassio is also something of an outsider in Venetian life – like Othello but less so – and it seems to rankle with Iago that both men have achieved more than him. Cassio is the only one of Iago's victims to remain alive at the end of the play.

Apart from Iago and those whose minds he poisons against him (like Montano and, later, Othello), all the other characters usually think well of Cassio. But Shakespeare has drawn a more rounded figure for us to see; Cassio's treatment of Bianca can be seen as heartless – or is he merely playing the man-about-town when he speaks laughingly of her to Iago, for the latter's benefit? But note how keen he is to keep Bianca's existence a secret from Othello, because he feels it will not advance his reputation. It is possible to see Cassio's polite and educated manner as somewhat forced – possibly even pompous – on occasions, as in his rather gushing speeches to Desdemona when he seeks her help. Like many of the characters in the play, there is more to Cassio than at first meets the eye and he is not wholly what he seems. This reinforces the play's underlying theme of the difference between appearance and reality.

## Emilia

Emilia

As Iago's wife and Desdemona's lady in waiting, Emilia links the two sides of Iago's plot. Eventually she also is instrumental in revealing her husband's malevolence, for which he stabs and kills her. At first Emilia unknowingly helps Iago by obtaining Desdemona's handkerchief, which he then secretes in Cassio's lodgings to use as evidence to Othello of Cassio's infidelity with Desdemona. Emilia seems not to wonder why Iago should want the handkerchief, perhaps because she tends not to concern herself with the more sophisticated thinking which seems to preoccupy and drive other characters.

Emilia is a very down-to-earth woman, whose matter-of-fact attitudes to marital infidelity form a sharp contrast to the very different – possibly unrealistically innocent – standards of her mistress. She is astute and wise to the ways of the world, as we see when she almost stumbles upon her husband's plot when she recognises (in Act 4, scene 2) that someone has lied to Othello 'to get some office'. Emilia's marriage seems unhappy – Iago jealously suspects her of infidelity with Othello – and she has an unflattering, if pragmatic, view of life and of men in general, which her husband's behaviour towards her appears to justify. She speaks her mind directly, without much evidence of forethought – unlike her husband, whose every word to other characters is carefully calculated for effect. At the end of the play her directness proves to be Iago's undoing, when she exposes his plotting without thought for the consequences. We can clearly see that whilst she might be a crude and vulgar character, Emilia is not wicked and has virtuous qualities such as honesty and loyalty to Desdemona. Like other characters, she cannot believe that anyone could be so determinedly evil as her husband has been, or that anyone could be prepared to go to such lengths for the sake of spite – something which protects Iago throughout. Nevertheless, as the character we might expect to be closest to understanding Iago's behaviour, she remains ignorant of her husband's plots until the very end, providing reinforcement for the play's underlying theme that in reality we know very little about other people.

## Bianca

Bianca

Although Bianca is not a major character in the play, she has an important part to play in relation to its major themes, especially that of appearance and reality and the way in which men see only the extremes of the whore (or devil) and the pure (or saintly). Iago speaks of her as a common prostitute: 'A housewife that by selling her desires/Buys herself bread and clothes.' But there is more to Bianca than this, for she has fallen in love with Cassio and is deeply offended at Emilia's accusation in Act 5, scene 2 that her relationship to him is nothing more than that of a common whore. Although Cassio and Iago exchange amused comments about Bianca's desire to wed Cassio, it seems as though he may have some feelings for her, although he is less than open with Iago about this and conceals her existence from Othello for fear that it might affect his reputation or professional advancement. Bianca's feelings towards Cassio seem genuine and she is jealous of another imagined suitor when he produces the handkerchief which, unknown to him, has been planted by Iago for him to find in his lodgings. Bianca's relationship with Cassio is almost a parallel to that of Roderigo and Desdemona, but for many characters in the play she represents the baser side of all women, who use their bodies as so much merchandise to sell, or as a means of gratifying their animal lusts. This is especially true of Iago, who uses this particular vision of womanhood as a means to achieve his ends. He persuades both Roderigo and Othello that Desdemona is driven by such emotions. Ironically, it is this very confusion between Bianca and Desdemona which Iago exploits when he arranges for Othello to overhear a conversation between himself and Cassio. Othello thinks they are talking about one woman when they are actually talking about the other.

## Brabantio

As a Venetian senator, Brabantio is upset to learn from Iago that his daughter Desdemona has eloped with Othello. He quickly becomes outraged by the crude sexual way in which the elopement is described, saying that it was foretold to him in a dream. He later expresses his disgust that his 'tender' and 'happy' daughter should have been seduced to Othello's 'sooty bosom'. He accuses Othello of having used magic charms and deceit to win his daughter's heart, but grudgingly accepts that this is not so when she publicly states her love for her husband.

Although Brabantio appears only in the first act and is not a major character, the incident with his daughter is significant in that it emphasises contemporary racist feelings towards Moors and underlines Othello's isolation from Venetian society. Brabantio's final words also anticipate Iago's arguments to Othello that Desdemona is deceitful by nature: 'She has deceiv'd her father, and may thee.' Later, we learn that Brabantio has died of grief because of his daughter's marriage, but not before he has engineered Othello's return from Cyprus to Venice. But it is interesting that Othello later (in Act 1, scene 3) explains that Brabantio actually encouraged his visits to Desdemona and looked forward to them himself, although it may be that it was only because he assumed that Othello would hold no attraction for her and he was therefore a 'safe' visitor, unlike the 'curled darlings' of Venetian society. It seems that Brabantio's mind has been poisoned by Iago's lewd suggestions, so that he can now only see Othello in a bad light. This refusal of Brabantio to change his mind once it is made up, even though (as he admits) he has no direct evidence to support his view, also anticipates the refusal of Othello to listen to Desdemona's pleading later in the play. It is not Desdemona who has deceived either of them, but they who have been blind to the truth.

# Main themes and images in *Othello*

**Darkness and light**

## Darkness and light

The symbolism of black and white is applied to skin pigmentation in a subtle way in the play. Iago has the black heart whilst the Moorish Othello, by his own admission, has a heart which 'nor set down aught in malice'; he has 'lov'd not wisely, but too well'. In contrast to this, a more straightforward role is taken by literal darkness and light in the play, also subtly, for it is connected to the other image of black/white and angel and devil. Notice, for example, that although three of the five acts occur during darkness or at night – with only Acts 3 and 4 being in bright daylight – it is during the daylight acts that the deceptions take place. During broad daylight, when Othello is certain that he is seeing things most clearly, the conversation between Iago and Cassio convinces him that Desdemona has been false to him, when in fact the two men are speaking about an altogether different woman – Cassio's admirer, Bianca. The play opens amidst confusion and darkness, a confusion which Iago is at pains to increase. At the start Othello's charismatic presence, together with the Duke's judicious carefulness, are enough to resolve the rising domestic and military disorder. By the time we reach Act 5, however, the clear judgement and measured manner of Othello has been destroyed, and the Duke is far away in Venice.

**Appearance and reality**

## Appearance and reality

The contrast between the way things are and the way they seem to be runs through many of Shakespeare's plays: in *Othello* this examination expands to encompass issues of conflict between good and evil which draw in almost all the characters. Until Iago poisons his mind, Othello seems to regard appearance and reality as identical; he is, for example, concerned that he and the world should do business at face value: 'my perfect soul shall manifest me rightly'. From the start, we find this set against the chameleon-like ability of Iago to blind others to his real nature; he comments to Roderigo 'I am not what I am'. Whilst Othello's 'perfect soul' lives behind a black face, Iago's black heart hides behind a smiling and seemingly honest white face. Only Iago truly seems to know the nature of the man within Othello, although he makes a fatal error in thinking that it is possible for him to keep hidden his own designs. As the tragedy unfolds, the darkness within Othello's soul comes increasingly to echo that of his appearance. Iago ironically describes himself as 'honest', but he is well aware of the kind of creature he is – unlike Othello, Cassio or the others, who think they see a genuinely honest figure in Iago.

Amongst the major characters, only in Desdemona do we see outward appearance reflecting inner character, appearance and reality as one, although she is continually suspected of being false. It is by persuading Othello of the likelihood of differences between appearance and reality that Iago steers him towards the final tragedy. As Othello's suspicions about his wife grow, his judgement declines. He becomes more willing to condemn and think ill of others – because ironically, he begins to take things exclusively at a particular face value. The construction of stereotypes and the corrosive effect they have on individual human judgement once they become accepted is one of the central issues of the play. Equally, the play concerns itself with many aspects of extreme 'opposites', such as darkness and light, cruelty and kindness, love and hate, greed and generosity, guilt and innocence.

## Love, jealousy, hatred

**Love, jealousy, hatred**

An important concern of the play is with the way love, jealousy and hatred can sometimes be so closely related that an individual's feelings can move from one to the other, whether their relationships are those of husband and wife or lady in waiting and mistress. Desdemona's feelings for Othello are straightforward and unchanging, but those of Othello himself are examined when under pressure from Iago. Feelings associated with broken trust, sexual betrayal, undervalued worth and unrewarded loyalty drive Iago himself, but are also found in other characters and the relationships between them.

When Cassio gives Bianca a handkerchief to work on, she at once becomes jealous and accuses him of having loved another. Emilia is uncompromising in her comments about the attractions of infidelity, of which the jealous Iago already suspects her. Othello becomes insanely jealous of Desdemona. All three relationships have in common the handkerchief and the central role played by the complete lack of actual evidence to support these feelings of betrayal. The relationships between Cassio and Bianca, and between Emilia and Iago, are characterised by the man's evident lack of complete regard for the woman throughout (unlike the relationship of Othello and Desdemona which is, at least at first, characterised by mutual love and respect). Notice that it is the relationship which represents the most elevated form of love which is made to fall, whereas we might feel that the others would have easily survived allegations of infidelity, given that one partner in each is already half convinced of it.

## Angel and devil

Angel and devil

Much of the play addresses itself to notions about the forces of good and evil, the way characters have within them aspects of angel and devil, and the relationship of these to Elizabethan notions of heaven and hell. At the start of the play the imagery used by other characters seeks to link Othello's actions with those of the devil – his appearance, his motives, even his use of witchcraft to win Desdemona's love. However, we see in Iago's soliloquy in Act 1 that he seeks to bring about the 'divinity of hell'. Several times in the play the nature of evil itself is explored and we are told that evil is most effective when masquerading as good. This is a common idea in Shakespeare: evil spreads by the corruption of good, by the poisoning of what is pure. In *Othello* this is achieved by the corrupting of *perceptions* of goodness and evil so that the angelic aspects of a character are the very things which become twisted against them. In Act 2, scene 3, Iago says of Desdemona that he will 'turn her virtue into pitch', in the same way that he vows to corrupt Othello's view of Cassio's public regard for her – he will 'catch him' in his 'own courtesies'. By the end of the play we find Othello referring to Desdemona as a 'fair devil': a word he uses increasingly often towards her as we approach the end of the play, although after her death it is Othello who thinks he will be tormented for what he has done: 'This look of thine will hurl my soul from heaven,/ And fiends will snatch at it'. He asks devils to whip him and calls upon fate to 'Blow me about in winds, roast me in sulphur,/Wash me in steep-down gulfs of liquid fire!'

At one level the play is a domestic tragedy about a husband and wife who are destroyed by a jealous underling, but the imagery and language show us that this is also the vehicle for a powerful exploration of the nature of good and evil. *Othello* explores the ambiguity between how things seem and what is real, but does so in a way which allows us to relate this to wider philosophical notions about the nature of good and evil and how reality is constructed, not by what we see, but by the way we think about it. *Othello* is an example of the recurrent interest of Shakespeare and his age in the nature of reality as perceived by humankind. This fascination also appears in *Hamlet*, when the hero observes that 'there is nothing either good or bad but thinking makes it so' and where the hero might have been speaking of Iago, rather than Claudius, when he notes 'that one may smile, and smile, and be a villain.'

# Text commentary

## Act 1 Scene 1

*Act 1 of the play takes place in Venice. Roderigo, a foolish Venetian gentleman who loves Desdemona, learns from Iago (whom he has been paying to help him court her) that she has eloped with Othello. Iago, Othello's aide, confesses that he hates his master because the position of Othello's Captain has been given to Cassio, when he feels that it should have been his by right. Iago says he is staying with Othello only in order to somehow gain revenge on him. Desdemona's father, Brabantio, who is a friend of Othello but does not know about the elopement, is woken and given the news about his daughter. Iago and Roderigo attempt to make Brabantio angry by discussing in crude terms the sexual conquest of his white daughter by the black Othello.*

**'Tush, never tell me, I take it much unkindly**
**That thou, Iago, who hast had my purse,**
**As if the strings were thine...'**

The play opens with Roderigo complaining about the way Iago has behaved;

Appearance and reality

significantly, their argument is about the betrayal of trust between two friends. This theme runs through the first act as next we hear Iago telling Roderigo how he will betray Othello because, he says, he has been passed over in promotion and feels let down. We then see Brabantio complaining about how his daughter Desdemona has deceived him by eloping with Othello. Many of the play's themes and images are introduced in this first scene: an interest in Othello's inner motivations (rather than his outward behaviour or deeds); the presence of secret loves and secret hates; the idea of deceiving others by poisoning their thoughts; references to night, to hell and the devil, to animals and – strongly running throughout the play – Iago's preoccupation with sexual behaviour and sexual imagery.

**'Thou told'st me thou didst hold him in thy hate.'**

Within half a dozen lines we are introduced to Iago's professed hatred of Othello and to the notion that Othello is a poor judge of the abilities and worth of others, as well as being proud and arrogant himself. Othello is much maligned at this point in the play, although not mentioned by name. As with the love of Desdemona for Othello, we are given a picture of them by others, but must wait for their appearance before we can begin to form our own conclusions.

Iago and Roderigo have come to the house of Brabantio to cause trouble

Othello

for Othello, whom they refer to as 'the Moor', 'the thick lips', 'an old black ram' and 'the devil'. The traditional imagery of white (good) and black (evil) is reversed in *Othello*, for the noble and cultivated hero who symbolises the forces of life-giving and order is black, whilst the scheming, murderous and base Iago is the (white) spirit of destruction.

### 'I follow him to serve my turn upon him...'

Iago says here that he 'follows' (serves) Othello only for his own destructive

Iago

ends. His resentment at Cassio being preferred over him has made him angry, perhaps in part because he has lost face and feels that he has been made to look foolish. Othello may, in Cassio, have made a sound appointment from a technical point of view but we might wonder why he chose not to appoint Iago. We are not told why this might be; perhaps Iago

is simply ungrateful and jealous of the advancement or good fortune of others and did not deserve the position himself, or his opinion of his own military qualifications may well be unrealistic. Whatever the reason, the situation has generated destructive forces and we see the same reaction from Brabantio and later Othello himself.

### 'I am not what I am.'

Iago openly admits that he adopts a deceiving exterior and uses others in order to achieve his own destructive ends. Ironically, Roderigo seems not to be paying sufficient attention to realise that Iago is behaving towards him in exactly the same way. He seems to be such a fool that Iago knows he can safely afford to tell him at least part of the truth. Appropriately, this scene takes place

Darkness
and light

at night, underlining the sense of concealment and confused perception which runs through the play. Much of the play's action occurs in darkness or gloom – evoking atmospheres of mystery, quietness and danger – and it is not until the start of Act 3 that daylight emerges briefly, before it dims in Act 4 and is extinguished again for Act 5. The gloominess of the present scene opens conspiratorially and ends in loud clamouring.

### 'Thou art a villain.'

Brabantio correctly identifies Iago's essential character with his first words.

Roderigo

It is Roderigo who now describes at length, if a little less coarsely than Iago, the circumstances of Othello's elopement with Desdemona. Notice how Roderigo is at pains to convince Brabantio that his daughter is with a 'knave', a 'lascivious Moor', and is happy to upset Brabantio because it helps his own cause. Brabantio is an important figure in Venetian society and can 'command at most' houses in organising a search. Othello is an important military figure on whom rests a significant part of the state's security and military capability. The tension between these two is not resolved until the end of the play. The strong racist perceptions which others have of Othello, so important later on, are introduced in the most sexually crude and inflammatory way. Roderigo is a willing participant in this scheme, as in all of Iago's other plots, but only so long as Iago is there at the start to strengthen his weak will.

The completely negative picture of Othello with which we have been presented has been skilfully given to characters who all have reason to be less than fair and balanced in their views. Iago has lost a promotion because of Othello's choice of Cassio, Roderigo feels deprived of the love of Desdemona because she has eloped with Othello, and Brabantio is encouraged to

Appearance and reality

believe that Othello has stolen his daughter away by force of charms and magic to seduce and violate her and give him beasts of the devil for grandchildren. In anticipation of the action of the rest of the play, it is significant that Brabantio is convinced of Iago's version of events, and infuriated into taking firm action by this, on the basis of very little in the way of hard evidence.

# Act 1 Scene 2

*Othello appears for the first time and is warned by Iago about Brabantio's anger. Cassio appears with a message from the Duke of Venice for Othello, who is to go to the Senate. Before Othello can respond to the Duke's summons Brabantio arrives, accuses Othello of using witchcraft to seduce his daughter and says he wishes him to be imprisoned and tried for stealing her. Brabantio decides to go with Othello to the Senate and raise his complaints there.*

### 'He...spoke such scurvy and provoking terms Against your honour...'

Iago tells Othello a particular version of the events we witnessed at the

opening of the play, suggesting that Brabantio spoke badly of Othello and that it was all Iago could do to prevent himself from killing Brabantio. Ironically, Iago says his 'conscience' will not let him behave this way, even though he has killed many men in war. As always, Iago is at pains to show himself in an 'honest' light, as a noble and loyal servant to everyone

Othello

he meets. Notice how Othello will not hide in his house or attempt to suppress the truth: ' 'Tis better as it is'. Othello says his actions and reputation will speak for him, for he is an honourable man, descended from royalty. This claim to royal ancestry would have had a considerable impact upon Shakespeare's audience; this, together with his black skin, makes the character of Othello a striking departure from anything seen before on the stage in this period.

## 'My parts, my title, and my perfect soul Shall manifest me rightly.'

Othello refuses to be inflamed by Iago's deliberate attempts to provoke a

Love, jealousy, hatred

confrontation between him and Brabantio. He has a substantial opinion of himself which, were it not echoed by many other characters, we might interpret as at least immodest, or at worst as dangerous pride. Do you feel that Othello's self-confidence is arrogance, or does it reflect a calm and rightful sense of his own worth? We may feel some anxiety that Othello places so much faith in the purity of his own character, when he is neither subtle nor particularly observant in his assessment of others. He comes to doubt his wife's evident loyalty yet trusts Iago implicitly, almost to the end. Interestingly, both Iago and Othello fatally overestimate their own qualities: one assumes he can completely control others, whilst the other's confidence in his frank and open nature is shown to be misplaced, for he has a dark and frightening side to his personality.

Appearance and reality

Many in Venice seem aware that Othello is visible from two different perspectives: he can be admired as an experienced soldier, a wise ambassador, a strong leader of others and a respected public figure; but as a man he is often regarded with the traditional contemporary hostility reserved for the stereotypical 'black' – he is a Moor and therefore ugly, sexually promiscuous and depraved, cruel and dangerous, and a practitioner of witchcraft who is closely allied with evil and the devil. Othello's own crisis of confidence, after Iago's poison has begun to work, is rooted in his awareness of these two sides to his public reputation and his private self-image. Ironically, however, it is Iago who here greets the visitors with a reference to Janus, the two-faced god. The group of men are led by Cassio and their talk about the comings and goings of messengers and the news of events from Cyprus emphasise the turmoil of activity in the night and are a dramatic echo of that begun by Iago.

The seeds of tragedy are sown when Othello starts to see Desdemona not as the individual person with whom he fell in love but as a typical stereotype of the deceiving Venetian woman; and begins to redefine himself in terms of a cultural stereotype, not in terms of an individual personality with the ability to make considered, reasoned judgements. The importance of judgement, of weighing all the evidence and not jumping to conclusions, is something to which our attention is later drawn in the behaviour of the Duke of Venice.

**'It is Brabantio. General, be advis'd,**
**He comes to bad intent.'**

Iago

Again Iago moves into action to try to ensure that a particular version of the situation is seen by others, this time by Othello. Iago frequently describes others and their motives in terms which in fact more accurately apply to him – here he is the one who has the 'bad intent'. Iago never misses an opportunity to cause confusion and to further his own malicious desire to see confrontation and violence. He even accuses his paymaster, Roderigo, of being behind the scurrilous rumours which Brabantio has believed and here publicly threatens to attack him with his sword. In contrast, Othello's cry of 'Keep up your bright swords, for the dew will rust 'em' emphasises his own essentially peaceful nature.

**'Hold your hands,**
**Both you of my inclining and the rest...'**

Othello

Again Othello orders that there be no fighting, emphasising his noble and civilised character and his calm and dignified manner, and contrasting it with those around him who too quickly give way to unruly passion and violence. It is ironic that Othello fails to take his own advice later in the play and yet that he should here note that 'were it my cue to fight, I should have known it'. This emphasises the importance, for the action of the play, of Othello's lack of recognition of the truth of what is before him and his misjudgement of when he should take action and when he should not.

# Act 1 Scene 3

*The Duke of Venice and his senators hear differing reports about what the enemy Turks seem to be planning. Two Turkish fleets have joined together and appear to be sailing towards the Venetian territory of Cyprus, which it seems they may invade. As the Duke considers how to respond to this situation, Othello enters, accompanied by Brabantio and their respective followers. Brabantio makes his complaint about his daughter's marriage and Othello responds. Desdemona is sent for to give her side of the story and supports Othello's defence that they are in love and that she married of her own free will. Brabantio reluctantly accepts Desdemona's account and the Duke returns to the Senate's previous business by ordering Othello to go immediately to Cyprus and take charge of the Venetian forces there. Desdemona is allowed to travel there also, but accompanied by Iago in a later ship. Roderigo despairs at losing Desdemona, but Iago says that she will soon regret her marriage to a Moor and may soon seek a lover. He adds that if Roderigo will come to Cyprus with them, Iago will continue to assist him by delivering gifts to Desdemona. After Roderigo leaves, Iago comments on how easily he extracts money from this foolish man and how he plans to revenge himself upon Othello and Cassio by making his master believe that Cassio is Desdemona's lover.*

## 'There is no composition in these news...'

The Venetian court's confusion about which of the conflicting reports they
 should believe is paralleled by that of the audience at this stage in the play, who have heard accounts of the behaviour and character of Desdemona and Othello but have as yet no direct evidence of their own. The behaviour of the Turks, traditionally cast as uncivilised, un-Christian and devious

**Angel and devil** enemies, is parallel to that of Iago. The audience of the period would sense the identification being made between the actions of Iago and the nature of the evil he commits; just as the Turks were believed to intend the destruction of Christendom, Iago too would be seen as an enemy of the true faith and an agent of the devil.

Throughout this scene – which effectively turns into the trial of Othello – the Duke is shown as a careful and cautious ruler, who closely examines all the evidence before committing himself to a particular conclusion, but who acts decisively thereafter. His careful weighing of the evidence acts as a strong contrast to Othello's behaviour later and acts as a model against which we may judge the other occasions later in the play when characters are tried and their honesty judged, always against evidence of a similarly contradictory or ambiguous nature.

## 'Rude am I in my speech,
## And little blest with the soft phrase of peace...'

Othello is a soldier, not a courtier, and is himself acutely conscious of this.
 He sees himself as straightforward and down to earth and is therefore at pains to dispel accusations that he used witchcraft or potions to win the love of Desdemona. However, as the action of the play unfolds, we see this man of decisiveness and action increasingly trapped within a tangle of mental confusion

**Othello** which echoes that with which this scene begins, with uncertainty about the actual number of ships and the true destination of the Turkish fleet.

Here, Othello contradicts his own courteous modesty at once by proving himself a measured, charismatic and effective speaker, reinforced later by his description of his courtship of Desdemona. Notice how, in contrast to Iago, Othello almost always speaks in verse, giving what he says an elevated, sincere and noble ring.

## 'A maiden never bold...'

Brabantio's description of his daughter's character at first sight seems at odds with what we see ourselves when Desdemona enters shortly after. But one of the play's themes is that people are not what they may appear to be; another is that people often see only what they wish to see in others. We also may understand that Brabantio retains a father's vision of his daughter and continues to see her as child-like long after she has matured beyond childish things. There are several points in the action of the play when the way men

and women perceive each other has an important effect on the action. It is also important at these places to consider how far these different perceptions are influenced – sometimes almost created – by the needs and wishes of the individuals holding them. For example, why might Brabantio wish (or need) to see Desdemona the way he does? Could it be parental nostalgia, or a matter of him being seen in public as a good

**Appearance and reality**

parent, with a 'respectable' and obedient family? This is another example in the play of one character misreading another, yet being certain that they actually understand them well. Try to decide what individual needs and wishes there might be in the make-up of Othello, Iago and Cassio which predispose them to take the particular views they do of themselves and other individuals.

## 'She lov'd me for the dangers I had pass'd, And I lov'd her that she did pity them.'

How much evidence is there in this scene to support Iago's contention that Othello is arrogant and proud? Notice how Othello seems almost to suggest that Desdemona courted him and that heaven has made him especially for her. It is useful to consider how Iago might have reported – say, to Roderigo – Othello's description of the way in which he and Desdemona fell in love.

We see here a sense in which Brabantio's accusation that 'witchcraft' was used to seduce his daughter might in some ways be right. Othello's past is romantic and adventurous and ranges across exotic foreign lands and peoples of which the Elizabethans were only newly becoming aware. This

**Angel and devil**

strangeness is emphasised by Othello's Moorish appearance.

Note that the Duke exercises restraint and balance in this first 'trial' scene in the play. Later, in the second such scene when Othello accuses Desdemona, we see how this restraint is absent in Othello's behaviour. Whilst the Duke here agrees that Desdemona be brought, as Othello requests, to give an account of whether or not the accusations of her father are true, Desdemona's plea that Cassio be brought and questioned about the handkerchief goes unheeded by Othello.

## 'I think this tale would win my daughter too...'

The Duke's comment signals two important aspects of Othello's account of his courtship of Desdemona. We see how Othello's 'round unvarnish'd tale', with its accounts of his exotic and adventurous past, is used by Shakespeare to tell the audience more about the main character and increase our sense of identification with him. We are also shown how Othello's open and straightforward account could indeed have attracted a well-bred young woman such as Desdemona, thus helping to counteract the assertions of Brabantio that her love could only have been won 'against all rules of nature' and by the use of 'some mixtures powerful o'er the blood,/Or with some dram conjur'd to this effect'. There is also another, more subtle point being made, for we see that Othello's courtship of Desdemona emphasises the power of words upon the feelings of others. It is by feigning the kind of honest exterior which Othello has, and by the skilful use of words, that Iago plants his destructive seeds into the minds of others.

Love, jealousy, hatred

This scene also shows us the wider world of political and military matters set against the love of Desdemona and Othello. These two aspects of the plot are woven together and connecting the fate of the lovers with the fate of the nation gives a wider, more universal setting to their bond which raises the final tragedy to a more heroic level. This also emphasises the pettiness of Iago and Roderigo and the spitefulness of Iago's motives.

### 'I do perceive here a divided duty...'

When we first meet Desdemona we find her – in contrast to what we have

Desdemona

been told so far – to be quiet, composed and assured, not at all the neurotic and lecherous, silly and headstrong young woman whom others have described. She also shows a clear grasp of her situation and is able and willing to answer for her own actions with clarity and maturity. Although she has entered into a marriage with an older man of another culture, she foresees no problems with this. Later, however, it is her ignorance of Othello's feelings of inadequacy and weakness which are partly responsible for the tragedy. Desdemona is no different from other characters in this respect – like them, she is unaware of the depths of the darker side of human nature. At the end of the play she seems to acknowledge this with her dying words, when she says that she was herself to blame for events.

### 'If virtue no delighted beauty lack,
### Your son-in-law is far more fair than black.'

The contemporary view of black people by many in Shakespeare's time was rooted in a popular stereotype which we might recognise today, although the Elizabethans regarded the holding of such an attitude far less censoriously than we do today. Nonetheless, Shakespeare is here exploring the way a

**Darkness and light**

reliance on external appearances can be very far off the mark – a notion which is at the heart of the tragedy later in the play. Othello is seen by the Duke as fair of heart, morally 'white'. Ironically, the measure which the Duke is using determines that Iago will be assumed by everyone to be fair of heart because of his white skin, in spite of his moral 'blackness'.

Notice how Shakespeare does not say that such stereotypes are completely wrong. He is being far more subtle than that in constructing the characters of both Othello and Iago in such a way that we can see elements of truth in the stereotype. Whilst we can recognise the stereotype and understand its power and persistence, we come to see that the passions which drive the major characters are beyond the reach of such simple devices to explain. Nowhere is this more so than in the character of Iago, whose degree of malevolence seems to bear very little relation to the extent of the wrongs which he imagines have been done to him by Othello and Cassio.

The Duke of Venice symbolises order and measured judgement in the play. Venice was at the time the most powerful commercial centre in the world, with a vast empire based on the wealth generated by shipping and trade. This is why Brabantio is outraged, in Scene 1, that anyone could think of robbery in such a civilised city and why, shortly, the action moves to an outpost of empire in Cyprus, where the restraining civility and culture of the Venetian court will be replaced by intrigue and baser passions.

### 'My life upon her faith: honest Iago...'

The play's two central ironies are encapsulated in this one line from Othello, where the certainty of his trust in Desdemona is set against his faith in Iago. His trust in the 'honest' Iago will open Othello's ears to the poison of his accusations, whilst Othello's life will indeed be forfeit as a result of his lack of faith in her loyalty.

### '...it is thought abroad, that 'twixt my sheets
### He's done my office; I know not if't be true...'

**Iago**

In Iago's first soliloquy he explains to the audience that although he has no proof of his wife's infidelity, he will behave as though it were true. This irrational state of mind anticipates the way Othello will be made to feel later in the play and gives us an insight into the malevolence of Iago. We also discover that Iago will use the positive character traits in Cassio and Othello to help him to destroy them: Cassio is a 'proper' (good looking/complete) man who is known to be attractive to women, whilst Othello has a 'free and open nature' and is willing to believe that men are honest if they appear to be so. Iago is confident that he will be able to lead them both 'by the nose'. However, just as Iago says of Othello and Cassio, this may attribute to Iago more than is his due. As you study the play you should consider the extent to which Iago is correct, but also how far Cassius and Othello are responsible for their own downfall. Or is Iago so skilful, so irresistible, that the disaster he plans for is completely unavoidable by the other characters?

## 'I ha't, it is engender'd; Hell and night
## Must bring this monstrous birth to the world's light.'

Earlier we saw how Brabantio accused Othello of being in league with the  devil in winning the love of Desdemona. In his soliloquy at the end of Act 1, Iago identifies himself with the forces of darkness and evil and the audience is shown the irrational hatred, sexual jealousy and envy which drive him. We see from this scene that it is not only jealousy of Othello which

Love, jealousy, hatred

drives Iago, for he says he will destroy Othello whether his suspicions about him are true or not. Iago is convinced that his is the superior understanding of human nature, all others being fools. He sees himself as more powerful and cunning than other men: this is an important part of his motivation.

# Self-test Questions Act One

**Uncover the plot**

Delete two of the three alternatives given, to find the correct plot. Beware possible misconceptions and muddles.

Roderigo/Brabantio/Lodovico loves Desdemona and has been paying Othello/Montano/Iago to help him court her. Iago confesses that he is jealous of/admires/hates his master. Desdemona's father, Montano/Brabantio/Cassio, does not know about her elopement and is woken and told about it. Othello is warned by Iago/Cassio/Emilia about his anger. Desdemona's father accuses Othello of using money/witchcraft/drugs to seduce his daughter. The Turkish fleets appear to be sailing towards the Venetian territory of Cyprus/Rhodes/Florence, which it seems they may invade. Desdemona's father makes his complaint about his daughter's marriage and Othello responds. Desdemona is sent for to give her side of the story and refutes/confuses/supports Othello's defence that they are in love. Her father accepts this, happily/indifferently/reluctantly. Desdemona is allowed to travel with/before/after her husband, accompanied by Iago/Cassio/Montano. Iago says that Desdemona will soon consummate/celebrate/regret her marriage to a Moor. Iago comments on how easily he extracts money from the foolish Roderigo/Brabantio/Lodovico and how he plans to revenge himself upon Othello and Brabantio/the Duke/Cassio by making his master believe that the latter is Desdemona's seducer/lover/admirer.

**Who? What? Why? When? Where? How?**

1   Who says of whom that they would not serve God even if the devil asked them to?
2   Whose description of Desdemona as 'a maiden never bold of spirit' seems in error?

3  Apart from the cannibals, which other two groups of exotic tribes did Othello tell Desdemona about?

4  What different numbers of ships are reported to be in the Turkish fleet?

5  Who says 'he is almost damn'd in a fair wife' and about whom?

6  Who says of whom that he was several times tempted to kill him for what he said about Othello?

7  Which character feels that he has foreseen present events in his dreams?

8  Who is encouraged to put money in his purse?

9  Of which character is it said that he 'thinks men honest that but seem to be so', and why is this an important comment?

10  Who says that who else is 'making the beast with two backs', and what does this mean?

## Who said that?

1  'Thou told'st me, thou didst hold him in thy hate.'

2  'Were it my cue to fight, I should have known it,/Without a prompter.'

3  'To vouch this is no proof,/Without more certain and more overt test.'

4  'I do perceive here a divided duty…'

5  ' 'tis in ourselves, that we are thus, or thus.'

6  'I think this tale would win my daughter too.'

7  'I will a round unvarnish'd tale deliver…'

8  'Even now, very now, an old black ram/Is tupping your white ewe.'

9  'Thou art a villain.'

10  'I know my price…'

## Open quotes

Identify the scene; complete the phrase; identify the speaker and the character being spoken to.

1  'But I will wear my heart upon my sleeve…'

2  'My parts, my title, and my perfect soul…'

3  'If virtue no delighted beauty lack,'

4  'And it is thought abroad, that 'twixt my sheets…'

5  'It is Brabantio, General, be advis'd,'

6  'She lov'd me for the dangers I had pass'd,'

7  'I follow him to serve my turn upon him:'

8  'Keep up your bright swords…'

9  'Look to her, Moor, have a quick eye to see:'

10  'Rude am I in my speech…'

# Act 2 Scene 1

*The action of the play has now moved to Cyprus. News arrives that the Turkish fleet has been scattered and perhaps destroyed by a storm raging out at sea. Cassio's ship arrives safely, followed by that bringing Desdemona, Iago, Emilia and Roderigo. Othello then arrives and is reunited with his wife. Iago tells Roderigo that Desdemona really loves Cassio, but says that she will love Roderigo when Cassio is disposed of. He persuades Roderigo to pick a fight with Cassio whilst he is on duty and thus disgrace him. Iago seems determined to believe that Othello has committed adultery with Emilia, his own wife.*

### 'Methinks the wind does speak aloud at land,
### A fuller blast ne'er shook our battlements...'

The storm which opens Act 2 forms a dramatic link with the action and passions of the preceding act, and also underlines the difference between Venice and Cyprus. The world of Venice is one characterised by civilised order and military and commercial might, a world ruled by a wise and thoughtful Duke. Cyprus may be an important strategic part of the Venetian empire but it is an outpost cut off from the values which Venice represents, surrounded by the dark powers of the Turkish enemy and beset by storms so powerful they seemed to flood the sky: 'The wind-shak'd surge, with high and monstrous main,/Seems to cast water on the burning bear,/And quench the guards of the ever-fixed pole'. The storm appears to have served Othello well, in dispersing the Turkish fleet and granting him a victory without a fight, but as a portent of the destruction to come it represents an ominous sign, emphasised in the ironic comment of Othello as soon as he appears: 'If after every tempest come such calmness,/May the winds blow, till they have waken'd death'. Later we see how the only calmness which appears after the storm within the lives of the main characters is indeed the calmness of death.

### 'Sir, would she give you so much of her lips
### As of her tongue she has bestow'd on me...'

Iago's opinion of all women is exposed here, as Cassio greets Emilia with a  kiss. When his wife objects that this is untrue, Iago elaborates on what he thinks women are, criticising them for behaving in ways which hide their real natures. Apart from the obvious irony of these comments, coming as they do from the arch deceiver in the play, they may also reveal something of the relationship between Iago and Emilia. Is Iago cold and callous towards his wife? Or are his bawdy comments to her here and elsewhere merely the outward signs of a happy, robust and earthy relationship?

Emilia

### 'He takes her by the palm; ay, well said...'

In this aside, Iago tells us how he will use the courteous nature of Cassio  against him by misrepresenting what it implies to a gullible Othello. Iago says of Cassio 'I will catch you in your own courtesies', making it clear that Iago knows as well as anyone that there is no real foundation for any suspicion. However, we should note that Cassio's 'courtesies' towards Desdemona are more akin to those of an Elizabethan poet-lover than those of a polite but disinterested courtier. Although there is a possibility that he has romantic affection for Desdemona – and possibly for many women, as a young man-about-town – there is no evidence that he behaves improperly towards her as a result.

Cassio

### 'That Cassio loves her, I do well believe it...'

This scene ends, like the last, with Iago plotting the undermining of others,

Iago

this time of Cassio. Roderigo is again Iago's dupe and the scene closes with another soliloquy from Iago in which we see his acknowledgement of the good qualities of Othello and Cassio, and his paranoid suspicion that his wife has slept with both of them. One source of Iago's suspicions seems to be his own feelings of lust towards Desdemona, for he assumes that other men are driven by the same base passions as he is, and thinks that only fools will deny this.

# Act 2 Scene 2

*A very short scene in which a gentleman reads a proclamation about the destruction of the Turkish fleet. This gives permission for great celebrations of the victory and of the consummation of Othello's marriage.*

### '...it is the celebration of his nuptials...'

The gentleman reads a proclamation in which it is stated that now that the

Angel and devil

Turkish fleet has been dispersed all is well, and that a time of celebration is at hand. Significantly, the garrison is given leave to relax, to lower its guard and take its ease. We should recall the connection already made between Iago and the Turks, for the enemy within – in several senses – is busily at work and will disturb the peace in several ways. The proclamation encourages every man to whatever 'sport and revels his mind leads him', reminding us of Iago's previous soliloquy and what he intends to do.

# Act 2 Scene 3

*Iago encourages Cassio to join the celebrations and makes him drunk and argumentative. When Cassio goes on duty he argues and fights with Roderigo. Iago tells Montano, the previous Governor of Cyprus, that Cassio is prone to drunkenness and fighting. Montano is convinced of this when Roderigo and a clearly drunken and quarrelsome Cassio appear. As he tries to separate the quarrelling men, Montano is wounded. Othello appears, having been disturbed by the noise, and Iago indicates that Cassio started the argument. Cassio is dismissed from his position by Othello. Iago encourages Cassio to seek Desdemona's help in persuading her husband to change his mind. Left alone, Iago says he will get Othello to misinterpret Desdemona's pleading for Cassio as evidence of her secret love for him.*

### 'She is a most exquisite lady.'

Not for the first time, we see a sharp contrast between the perceptions of Iago and those of Cassio. To Cassio, Desdemona is a 'fresh and delicate creature'

Iago

who although 'inviting' in her manner is also 'right modest' and one who has a voice of 'perfection'. Iago, on the other hand, characteristically sees her in baser terms as 'sport for Jove' and 'full of game', with a look which is pure 'provocation' and a voice which is 'an alarm to love'. The way Iago inflames men by his graphic and base descriptions of sexual intercourse reflects a feature of his own preoccupation. Here it echoes the way he spoke to Brabantio at the start of the play.

### 'Not to-night, good Iago; I have very poor and unhappy brains for drinking...'

Cassio says he wishes someone would invent some other way in which people could entertain themselves apart from drinking, because it affects him badly; he is 'unfortunate in the infirmity' and 'dare not task' his weakness with any more wine, having already drunk some that night. Iago is determined to get Cassio drunk because he is supposed to be on duty that night and Iago has arranged for Roderigo to meet Cassio – seemingly by chance – and to quarrel, so that Cassio will be disgraced. This is a necessary dramatic device, so that Cassio's attempts to regain favour with Othello with the help of Desdemona will later provide the opportunity for Iago to corrupt Othello's mind with suggestions of his wife's collusion and infidelity with Cassio. Iago here adopts the same tactic he will later use on Othello, that of finding a person's weakness and then exploiting it under the guise of being a loyal friend.

Cassio

Cassio's drunkenness is comic in its effect and it seems clear that Shakespeare expected the actor to play as comedy the lines where Cassio insists that he is not drunk, together with his declaration that he 'can stand well enough, and speak well enough'. This and Cassio's 'this is my right hand, and this is my left hand' are clear opportunities for the audience to enjoy his drunken confusion and lack of proper co-ordination. But you should notice the ironic parallel in this scene, in which Cassio's loss of physical control and of his reputation anticipate the more extreme version of the same situation in which Othello will later find himself. Othello loses his reputation, and more, following his loss of physical and mental control of his circumstances.

### 'And let me the cannikin clink, clink...'

The drinking and singing in this scene is a familiar part of Shakespeare's plays. As well as providing broad humour and amusement for the audience, this interlude forms a dramatic contrast with the following episode of the fight, Othello's fury and Cassio's dismissal from office. We see Cassio persuaded to drink beyond what he knows to be sensible – especially for a man with his own confessed sensitivity to it – in a way which we recognise as a familiar feature of humanity.

### 'And 'tis a great pity that the noble Moor
### Should hazard such a place as his own second...'

Montano's comment here about Cassio's alleged habitual drunkenness is ironic, for although he speaks of Cassio, the audience can see that accusations of having an 'ingraft infirmity' apply more closely to Iago. Later, after the fight when Montano is too hurt to give any explanation, we see how Iago is left to provide Othello with the story of how the brawl began and to put his particular gloss on events.

### 'Are we turn'd Turks, and to ourselves do that
### Which heaven has forbid the Ottomites?'

Othello accuses the brawlers of bringing upon themselves the very destruction of peace and order which the storm prevented the Turks inflicting. He therefore links the brawl with imagery of self-destruction and the behaviour of barbarians.

### 'Now by heaven
### My blood begins my safer guides to rule...'

Othello

Othello's comment is telling in a way he does not know, for it anticipates the way he increasingly will come to behave and exposes the weakness which Iago will exploit. Othello is angry at the disturbance of the peace and calls upon Iago to explain. We see how the Moor is capable of powerful emotions which his outwardly calm exterior usually conceals and this helps to prepare us for his passion in Act 4.

Appearance and reality

Notice how Iago plays the part of one from whom the truth has to be dragged because of his loyalty to Cassio. By seeming to admit only what is wrung from him, Iago gives the impression that things are in fact much worse than he is prepared to admit, that he is putting the best possible face on things so as to minimise the wrong that has been done. Later Iago will use this to great effect when describing the relationship between Cassio and Desdemona to Othello in such a way as to suggest adultery. Her entry at this point may have suggested this plot to Iago, for he is nothing if not wonderfully adept at improvising, so as to exploit any opportunity for further mischief to the full.

### '... reputation is an idle and most false imposition...'

Iago frequently mixes truth, half-truth and outright lies to achieve his ends. Here he speaks the truth about 'reputation' in a way which only he and the

Cassio

audience can fully appreciate. He plants the notion in Cassio's mind that Desdemona would be his best ambassador to ply his suit with Othello, knowing that this will further his own scheming. Notice how the drink has affected Cassio so that he remembers little of the brawl. He curses drink as an 'enemy' which men put in their mouths 'to steal away their brains'. In a similar way Iago puts 'pestilence' into the ears of every character he meets, thus to steal away their reason. By the end of the play Othello will fall senseless to the ground in a way which echoes Cassio's behaviour; so different from his normal self that he can barely recognise who he has become or what he has done.

### 'When devils will their blackest suits put on, They do suggest at first with heavenly shows...'

The identification of Iago with the spirits of hell is reinforced in this soliloquy,

Angel and devil

where he gloats over his ploy to get Cassio to persuade Desdemona to speak to Othello on his behalf. This will allow Iago to 'turn her virtue into pitch' in Othello's eyes. The use of oxymoron ('Divinity of hell') adds impact to Iago's evil, couched as it is in the form of one of the frequent oaths which Iago utters, many of which refer to bestial, sexual or evil things and thus reflect the general tenor of his thinking. The scene ends with Iago determining to use his own wife as part of his plot.

## Self-test Questions Act Two

**Uncover the plot**

Delete two of the three alternatives given, to find the correct plot. Beware possible misconceptions and muddles.

The action of the play has now moved to Rhodes/Florence/Cyprus. News arrives that the Turkish fleet has been scattered/turned away/sunk. Iago/Othello/Cassio tells Roderigo that Desdemona really loves Brabantio/Cassio/Lodovico but says that she will love him soon. Othello/Roderigo/Iago is persuaded to pick a fight with Cassio whilst he is on duty and thus disgrace him. Iago/Cassio/Montano seems determined to believe that Othello/Roderigo/Lodovico has committed adultery with Emilia. A great celebration is held to honour the occasion/consummation/anniversary of Othello's marriage. Iago gets Cassio/Othello/Roderigo drunk and argumentative. Montano/Iago/Cassio argues and fights with Roderigo/Othello/Bianca. Emilia/Iago/Othello tells Montano that Cassio/Brabantio/Roderigo is prone to drunkenness and fighting. As he tries to separate a quarrel, Roderigo/Iago/Montano is wounded. Cassio/Iago/Montano is dismissed from his position by Othello. Roderigo/Iago/Emilia encourages him to seek Desdemona's help in persuading Othello to change his mind. Left alone, Cassio/Roderigo/Iago says he will get Othello to misinterpret this.

### Who? What? Why? When? Where? How?

1 Which character thinks of which other that he may be relished 'more in the soldier than the scholar'?
2 Who describes Othello as having 'a constant, loving, noble nature'?
3 Which character has love 'turn'd almost the wrong side outward'?
4 Who has 'poor and unhappy brains for drinking'?
5 Who thinks that Othello should be told about Cassio's 'infirmity'?
6 Who complains to whom that his money is almost spent?
7 Whose virtue is to be turned to pitch?
8 Who is 'sport for Jove', according to whom?
9 Which character is sure he knows his left hand from his right?
10 Who describes whom as 'poor trash of Venice'?

### Who said that?

1 'As little a web as this will ensnare as great a fly as Cassio.'
2 'Sir, he is rash, and very sudden in choler...'
3 'Are we turn'd Turks...'
4 'I ha' been to-night exceedingly well cudgel'd.'
5 'Well, happiness to their sheets!'
6 'What wouldst thou write of me, if thou shouldst praise me?'
7 '...the man commands like a full soldier.'
8 'I fear Cassio with my night-cap...'
9 'My blood begins my safer guides to rule...'
10 '...that men should put an enemy in their mouths, to steal away their brains.'

### Open quotes

Identify the scene; complete the phrase; identify the speaker and the character being spoken to.

1 'Sir, would she give you so much of her lips...'
2 'If after every tempest come such calmness'
3 '...reputation is an idle and most false imposition...'
4 'Come on, come on, you are pictures out o' doors;/Bells in your parlours; wild-cats in your kitchens;'
5 'O, you are well tun'd now,/But...'
6 'I am not drunk now, I can stand...'
7 'Thy honesty and love doth mince this matter,/Making it light to Cassio'
8 'Reputation, reputation...'
9 'When devils will their blackest sins put on,'
10 'There's none so foul, and foolish thereunto,'

# Act 3 Scene 1

*Cassio has arranged for some musicians to serenade Othello and Desdemona the morning after their nuptial celebrations. A clown is sent down to pay the musicians to depart, as they are disturbing the married couple. Cassio persuades the clown, in a conversation full of lewd double-meanings, to give a message to Emilia, Desdemona's lady-in-waiting. Iago arrives and says he will get Emilia to see Cassio at once and will also distract Othello so that Cassio may speak freely with Desdemona. Emilia tells Cassio that his problems may soon be solved, as Desdemona has already begun to intercede on his behalf, but nevertheless agrees to arrange a meeting between him and Desdemona.*

### 'You ha' not been a-bed then?'

Iago's entrance and comment to Cassio help to emphasise the continuous

flow of time in the drama. At one level the time scheme of the play, encompassing all the action within two days, emphasises the headlong rush of the tragedy and the seemingly irresistible progress of Iago's evil plans. The other, unspoken, time scheme is that assumed by the audience; one which will allow sufficient time for the action of the play to have taken place – where, for example, Desdemona is alleged to have committed

**Darkness and light**

adultery with Cassio several times. However, the dramatic reality of the play is that the flow of time both accelerates and slows down as dictated by the playwright. The inconsistencies in the time scheme of the play are not noticed by the audience, who respond only to the flow of the action before them.

### 'The General and his wife are talking of it, And she speaks for you stoutly...'

Before Cassio has had time to ask Desdemona to intercede with Othello on his behalf, she is already doing so. Thus the natural actions of Iago are exploited by him to their own detriment. In this scene we meet Emilia for the first time and see that she is a close companion of Desdemona, being allowed to remain whilst such matters are discussed.

**Desdemona**

## Act 3 Scene 2

*A very brief scene in which we see Othello discharging his public duties as Governor of Cyprus and going off to inspect the island's fortifications.*

### 'This fortification, gentlemen, shall we see't?'

Although this very brief scene marks the passing of time, it is also used by Shakespeare to develop another important dramatic irony within the action. Whilst Othello devotes his time to the proper execution of his military responsibilities – inspecting the fortifications which secure the island against external attack – he is unaware of the greater danger from Iago's attack within his own domestic life.

**Appearance and reality**

## Act 3 Scene 3

*Desdemona tells Cassio that she will do everything she can to persuade Othello to reinstate him. Othello and Iago arrive and Desdemona pleads with her husband. Othello agrees to her request, but after she has left Iago makes it clear to Othello that he has something on his mind about Cassio which he would rather not discuss. Othello asks him to say what is on his mind and before he departs Iago skilfully steers Othello's feelings towards jealousy about Cassio's relationships with Desdemona. When Desdemona and Emilia reappear, Desdemona thinks her husband seems unwell. Othello and Desdemona depart and Emilia picks up a handkerchief – Othello's first present to his wife – which Desdemona has unknowingly dropped. Emilia gives the handkerchief to Iago, who says he will leave it in Cassio's lodgings so as to fuel Othello's suspicions further. Othello returns, almost completely convinced of Desdemona's unfaithfulness, but demanding proof. Iago says Cassio has talked in his sleep about his love for Desdemona and that Iago has seen him wiping his beard with her handkerchief. Othello believes Iago and plans his revenge. He tells Iago to murder Cassio and says he will kill Desdemona himself.*

### 'Ha, I like not that.'

Iago plants a seed which he will nurture throughout this scene. He suggests

Cassio

that the figure he has seen leaving cannot be Cassio, because he is an honourable man who would not stoop to such a sneaking and dishonest kind of behaviour. By suggesting that an action which might seem innocent may in reality conceal something altogether more suspicious, he hints that Cassio has a guilty conscience and then later suggests to Othello what it might be that Cassio could feel guilty about. Iago proceeds with stealth, using insinuation rather than outright lies to achieve his ends. Even Iago's revelation at the end of this scene about Cassio's dream *may* be the truth, but by then it is too late for Othello to see it as anything but 'proof' of his wife's adulterous affair.

### 'As where's that palace, whereinto foul things Sometimes intrude not?'

Iago

Iago speaks of how the purest soul may suffer the intrusion of foul things at times. This echoes exactly what is happening in this scene, where Iago pours his foul poison into the mind of Othello.

### 'Though I perchance am vicious in my guess...'

Iago again uses the extremely effective device of appearing to be very

Appearance and reality

reluctant to speak ill of others whilst at the same time managing to suggest that he knows much which would distress Othello if he were to tell him about it. No matter how many dreadful things Iago then says, Othello is left with the abiding belief that he knows more terrible things than he has told and is trying to minimise the hurt to his master, because of his honest friendship and regard for him. We see how cleverly Iago uses this device here in actually telling Othello the real truth that he invents 'faults that are not' and that it 'were not for your quiet, nor your good,/Nor for my manhood, honesty, or wisdom,/To let you know my thoughts.'

## 'Who steals my purse, steals trash, 'tis something, nothing, 'Twas mine, 'tis his, and has been slave to thousands...' ll  1 6 0

Othello reaches his low point in this scene, for he is threatened in his most

Othello

vulnerable area – his reputation. Iago is skilful, as always, in seeming to know more than he tells and in appearing to speak only under pressure from Othello. Here Iago advances the opposite argument to Othello as he did to Cassio, now saying that reputation is everything. Notice how he next advises Othello to beware of being jealous, thereby cleverly planting the idea of being jealous in his mind. He adopts the same approach when raising the suggestion of Desdemona's adultery.

## 'I speak not yet of proof...'
## Look to your wife, observe her well with Cassio'

Iago skilfully twists his words so that the fact of Desdemona's adultery appears

Desdemona

not to be in doubt – only the proof of it, which will soon be forthcoming. Iago capitalises on Othello's inexperience of Venetian customs when he says 'I know our country disposition well', further encouraging Othello to believe his lies by pointing out how Desdemona has already deceived her father in marrying him. This echoes Brabantio's final words in

Act 1, scene 3: 'She has deceived her father, and may thee.' This episode also reinforces our sense of Othello's important dramatic status as an 'outsider', someone so unfamiliar with Venetian customs and society that Iago's lies will seem plausible, and who will accept as true the suggestion that all Venetian women routinely commit adultery. Othello's experience is limited to vast deserts, strange races 'whose heads/Do grow beneath their shoulders', and of the battlefield.

On the other hand, we must be careful not to see Othello simply as an

Iago

uninformed and gullible fool, for Shakespeare is showing us how all people base their judgements of others on what are really very shaky foundations. This proves to be as true for Iago as for any other character, and we should beware of accepting the worm's eye view of human dignity which Iago has as being any more correct than Othello's. For the

audience, Iago's determination to see the baser possibilities in the motives of others means that it becomes impossible for us to see any of the characters with innocent eyes. We are made unwilling accomplices in Iago's scheming because we are repeatedly reminded of a particular perspective on human nature. Whilst we might deplore Iago's evil and destructive behaviour, it is difficult not to admire the skill and creativity with which he achieves his ends.

Iago's mention of the possibility of providing Othello with 'proof' should

Appearance and reality

remind us of how this absolute notion has been used so far in the play. There have been no occasions when proof, in the legal sense, has been forthcoming, and we see how skilfully Iago exploits the necessity for characters to act without absolute proof on many occasions. For example, how certain have we – or characters within the play – been of the sincerity of Iago's support for Roderigo's courtship of Desdemona, the bewitchment of Desdemona by Othello, the destination of the Turkish fleet, the fleet's permanent departure, or the dereliction of Cassio in his duty? It is this ambiguity about 'proof', and the way it is so often a matter of how things are seen, which allows Iago to move the criteria for Desdemona's guilt onto such a little thing as the handkerchief.

## 'Haply, for I am black,
## And have not those soft parts of conversation...'

We have had several opportunities by now to see into the mind of Iago

Othello

through his soliloquies, but this is the first soliloquy given to Othello. This allows the audience to see something which it has not been dramatically necessary for them to see until now: the inner workings of Othello's mind. Iago's outward appearance and inner thoughts have always been very different and we have needed to appreciate this in order to fully understand the action, but until this point the inner workings of Othello's character have mirrored his outward appearance. In this scene – the turning point of the action and the longest in the play – this correspondence between outward appearance and inner reality in the way Othello is seen by other characters breaks down. This becomes most noticeable from Desdemona's viewpoint.

Othello dwells upon what he has come to see as his deficiencies in the eyes

Appearance and reality

of others. The suggestion is that Desdemona may well see him this way: as a black man who is getting old and who has few of the civilised graces of more sophisticated men. Desdemona enters and is concerned that her husband seems unwell – which is true, but not in the way she thinks, for he is sick of spirit, not of body. This episode also gives Emilia the opportunity to pick up Desdemona's dropped handkerchief, which she intends to have copied for her husband, Iago. We might reasonably conclude that Emilia does not intend to keep the handkerchief for good.

### 'I will in Cassio's lodging lose this napkin,
### And let him find it.'

In this soliloquy, Iago reveals the key to his success; it is Othello's weakness which will bring about his own destruction. Iago is closely identified with the powers of hell at several points in the play; notice here how he refers to 'the mines of sulphur', echoing the traditional image of hellfire.

Angel and devil

### 'I think my wife be honest, and think she is not,
### I think that thou art just, and think thou art not...'

Here we see Othello wavering between suspicion and loyalty as he struggles

with himself to determine the truth. This proves to be an important turning point for Othello, whose character is such that he finds it difficult to release a notion once it is formed in his mind. He replaces his existing image of Desdemona only with great difficulty, both here and when he reverses it once more at the end of the play. In desperation he demands

Othello

certainty – and here we see the fatal weakness in his make up. The love of Othello and Desdemona has been cast from the start in terms of the absolutes of devotion and purity of passion. Other characters recognise the world they inhabit as one where the base and the noble can exist side by side in themselves and in others. Othello's vision of himself and his wife excludes such compromise, and so when Iago eventually offers Othello 'proof' he is savage in the passion with which he believes her to be guilty.

Othello's status as a tragic hero depends upon how we interpret his behaviour here. Some commentators offer this passage in the play as evidence of Othello's pettiness, instability and suspicious nature, although it may equally be offered as evidence of his feelings of vulnerability, his sense of isolation and inferiority. Equally, we may decide that what we see here is evidence of Iago's mastery of intrigue and deception, which reflects on the essential character of Othello only in a slight way. Othello may be seen as a noble and heroic figure who brings about his own destruction by one fatal error of judgement, or at the other extreme as little more than an arrogant and proud figure who, like Brabantio, is duped by a clever and devious liar. What you decide will depend on the evidence which you cite in answering the important question: why does Othello believe Iago?

### 'Give me a living reason, that she's disloyal.'

Iago realises that he has awakened Othello's wrath and that if he cannot support his suggestions of Desdemona's infidelity he will pay dearly for it. At this point it is interesting to consider whether Iago is thinking rapidly on his

Iago

feet, or has prepared his answer beforehand as he tells Othello about Cassio talking in his sleep. Othello is by now so desperate to be certain one way or the other that he seems almost keen to pounce upon Iago's account as true. Ironically, the roles of these two characters are briefly changed when it is Othello who is convinced of Desdemona's betrayal and Iago who is arguing in support of Cassio that 'this was but his dream'. Othello's passion has now overtaken Iago's plotting and sweeps the action along.

### 'Do not rise yet.'

In a bizarre parody of religious devotion, Iago kneels with Othello as they swear a 'sacred vow' to seek 'black vengeance' against Desdemona and

Angel and devil

Cassio. We also see how the language of Iago and Othello has been interchanged with their roles. Iago is now clearly the master in the relationship, as the villain speaks of vows to heaven, of service and obedience whilst Othello, using language more appropriate to Iago, says of Desdemona: 'Damn her, lewd minx' and calls her a 'fair devil'.

# Act 3 Scene 4

*Desdemona is asking Emilia about the whereabouts of her handkerchief when Othello arrives and asks his wife for the handkerchief, saying it has special magical powers and must never be lost. Desdemona says it is not lost and tries to change the subject to the reinstatement of Cassio. Othello becomes furious at this and leaves. Iago and Cassio arrive and when they are told about Othello's fury Iago goes after him, saying he will find out what is the matter. Desdemona and Emilia leave also and, whilst waiting for Iago's return, Cassio is visited by Bianca, his mistress, who gently scolds him for not visiting her more often. Cassio asks Bianca to copy an embroidered handkerchief he has found in his lodgings and says he will visit her soon.*

### 'Is he not jealous?'

The clown begins Scene 4 as a dramatic interlude between the last scene and

Love, jealousy, hatred

that of this, closely followed by this ironic conversation between Emilia and Desdemona, who is seeking her handkerchief. Disaster is about to strike at the moment when Desdemona feels most secure. She is certain that Othello has no jealousy within him, as in the place of his birth the sun 'drew all such humours from him'. Othello's comment about Desdemona's 'moist' palm echoes a contemporary belief that this indicated lustful desires, and shows us that he is already predisposed to look for evidence to support his belief that she is unfaithful.

### 'The handkerchief!'

We do not know whether Othello's comments about the magical properties of the handkerchief reflect what he really believes, or are just a device to inflate its importance for his purposes here. However, notice how the idea of Othello having used witchcraft to woo Desdemona surfaces again here and serves to remind us once more of his status as an 'outsider' and also to suggest that he is now becoming identified with the dark forces of superstition and evil. These are evidence of the changes which Iago has brought about in him.

Why does Desdemona lie about the whereabouts of the handkerchief?

*Desdemona*

This is one of the key moments of the play, where the absolute truth from Desdemona *might* have averted disaster, but it passes ungrasped. Perhaps she avoids telling Othello because she does not wish to hurt his feelings; the handkerchief might yet turn up. Perhaps she is frightened by seeing a hitherto unknown and aggressive side of her husband's character. Perhaps she is genuinely hurt at the over-importance he places upon such a little thing. Attempting to deflect the conversation onto the matter of Cassio's reinstatement only makes things much worse. Whichever way it goes, it seems, Iago wins.

### 'Tis not a year or two shows us a man:
### They are all but stomachs, and we all but food...'

*Emilia*

Emilia at once recognises that Othello's temper is fuelled by jealousy. Her more realistic measuring of human nature reflects her more matter-of-fact approach to life than that of her mistress. Emilia sees both good and bad in people (mostly bad) but accepts this as the way of the world, whereas Desdemona is astonished at this unusual behaviour from her husband.

### 'They are not ever jealous for the cause,
### But jealous for they are jealous...'

Emilia puts her finger on the danger which Desdemona now faces. She knows, from her broader experience of life, that there is no protection for Desdemona in her assertion that she never gave Othello cause to be jealous. Jealousy is a self-propelled emotion which fuels itself upon its own existence, not necessarily upon the truth. Typically, Desdemona puts Othello's outburst down to worries about matters of state, not the base emotion of jealousy.

### 'Throw your vile guesses in the devil's teeth,
### From whence you have them; you are jealous now...'

Cassio's relationship with Bianca is clearly more than a simple one of customer and prostitute, which is how several other characters see her. On

Bianca

several occasions when they meet, Cassio speaks to her kindly and with affection and their relationship is a less elevated and more down-to-earth version of that between Othello and Desdemona. However, we see in Act 4, scene 1 that when Cassio speaks to Iago about Bianca he laughs at the suggestion that their relationship is serious and calls her a 'bauble' who has convinced herself that he will marry her. You may feel that Shakespeare left the relationship between Cassio and Bianca deliberately ambiguous, offering the audience the possibility that Cassio is an experienced and worldly man. But there is no evidence in the play that Cassio is in any way improper in his relationships with either Desdemona or Bianca. Notice how the handkerchief has provoked another heated exchange – this time from a woman's perspective – about unwarranted jealousy.

# Self-test Questions Act Three

### Uncover the plot
Delete two of the three alternatives given, to find the correct plot. Beware possible misconceptions and muddles.

Cassio/Iago/Othello has arranged for some musicians to serenade Othello and Desdemona the morning after their nuptial celebrations. Iago/Roderigo/Gratiano arrives and says he will get Bianca/Desdemona/Emilia to see Cassio at once and will also distract Othello so that they may exchange gifts/speak freely/plan their elopement. Desdemona has already begun to love/plead for/miss Cassio. Emilia/Desdemona/Bianca pleads with Othello on Cassio's behalf. Iago skilfully steers Othello's feelings towards jealousy/anger/murder about Cassio's relationships with Desdemona. Bianca/Cecilia/Emilia picks up a handkerchief – Othello's wedding/first/engagement present to Desdemona – which she has unknowingly dropped. She gives the handkerchief to Iago/Roderigo/Montano. Iago tells Othello that Cassio has talked to him/to Bianca/in his sleep about his love for Desdemona and that Iago has seen him wiping his face/eyes/beard with her handkerchief.

Othello asks Desdemona for the handkerchief, saying it was his mother's/has special magical powers/is needed to be copied. Desdemona says it is at home/in her luggage/not lost. Othello becomes furious/accepts this/says it does not matter. Cassio is visited by Bianca/Emilia/Cecilia, his mistress/sister/cousin, who gently scolds him for not visiting her more often. Cassio asks her to keep/copy/have a handkerchief he has bought/been given/found.

### Who? What? Why? When? Where? How?
1   What is spotted with strawberries?
2   Who, in this act, says he is made 'poor indeed' if he is robbed of his good name?
3   Who often accompanied Othello when he went to woo Desdemona?
4   How does the handkerchief get into Cassio's lodgings?
5   Who was going to who else's house when she met him on her way to his?
6   Which characters kneel together in this act?

7　From whom does Othello say his mother originally got the handkerchief?
8　Why are the musicians sent away?
9　According to Iago, why was he awake to hear Cassio talk in his sleep about Desdemona?
10　Who gives Iago the handkerchief and where does she get it from?

**Who said that?**
1　'I cannot think it,/That he would sneak away so guilty-like...'
2　'Who steals my purse, steals trash...'
3　'My wayward husband hath a hundred times/Woo'd me to steal it.'
4　'... give me the ocular proof.'
5　'I do beseech thee, grant me this,/To leave me but a little to myself.'
6　'They are not ever jealous for the cause,/But jealous for they are jealous.'
7　'... you are jealous now/That this is from some mistress.'
8　'Throw your vile guesses in the devil's teeth.'
9　'I speak not yet of proof.'
10　'... and when I love thee not,/Chaos is come again.'

**Open quotes**
Identify the scene; complete the phrase; identify the speaker and the character being spoken to.
1　'Be thou assure'd, good Cassio, I will do...'
2　'Haply, for I am black,/And have not those soft parts of conversation...'
3　'... trifles light as air/Are to the jealous, ...'
4　'I think the sun where he was born...'
5　'The general and his wife are talking of it, ...'
6　'I think my wife be honest, and think she is not,'
7　'As where's that palace, whereinto foul things...'
8　'They are all but stomachs ...'
9　'I had rather be a toad,'
10　'O, beware jealousy;/It is the ...'

# Act 4 Scene 1

*Iago tells Othello that Cassio has admitted committing adultery with Desdemona and inflames Othello's passions with lurid descriptions. Othello collapses in a faint and Iago gloats over his success. When Othello recovers, Iago suggests that he eavesdrop on a meeting between him and Cassio when he will overhear Cassio talking about Desdemona. Othello agrees, but in the conversation Iago talks to Cassio about Bianca, his lover, although Othello thinks that Cassio's disrespectful and coarse conversation is about Desdemona. As Othello continues to secretly observe Cassio, Bianca arrives, angry that the handkerchief Cassio has given her belongs to another woman. Othello now thinks that Cassio has given Desdemona's token of her love for him to a common prostitute. Othello vows to kill Desdemona and Iago says he will kill Cassio that night. Lodovico arrives from Venice to say that Othello must return and that Cassio is to govern Cyprus in his absence. Desdemona says she is pleased with this news and Lodovico is astonished when Othello beats her for this and then humiliates her in front of him. After Othello leaves in a rage, Lodovico is told by Iago that Othello's behaviour is, these days, often much worse than this.*

### 'To be naked with her friend abed,
### An hour, or more, not meaning any harm?'

Again we join a scene part-way through a conversation, is a device which

Shakespeare uses several times in this play to engage our attention and increase the tension. Iago is now much bolder than before, because he has passed the dangerous moment when Othello swayed between trust in his wife's fidelity and suspicion of her honour. Iago now poisons Othello's mind with pictures of his wife in bed with Cassio, then attempts to persuade him that this may be but innocent pleasure.

Appearance and reality

Understandably enough, Othello finds this suggestion preposterous, but we should note how skilfully Iago allows Othello's imagination to do his dirty work for him.

### 'Lie with her, lie on her?'

Othello falls prey to Iago's evil influence. He rejects the possibility of trusting

his own feelings of love for Desdemona and is instead seduced by Iago's jealousy and evil. Notice how Iago is subtly identified with satanic evil at several points in the play, as here when Othello cries 'O devil!' and falls down. Iago, indifferent to Othello's condition, immediately replies 'Work on,/My

Angel and devil

medicine, work.' The calm and rational Othello of the earlier scenes is now completely gone and we see contrasted Othello's mental torture and Iago's unfeeling reaction to it.

### 'Stand you awhile apart,
### Confine yourself but in a patient list'

Iago tells Othello to conceal himself so that he may overhear for himself the

tale of how Cassio committed adultery with Desdemona. Othello's willingness to indulge in spying is another mark of the depths to which he has already sunk. Iago says that Cassio regards his sexual intercourse with Desdemona as a matter for 'jeers', 'gibes, and notable scorns', suggesting that he has

Othello

treated her – and that she has behaved – as less than a common prostitute. This echoes Roderigo and Iago's original suggestion to Brabantio, that his daughter had run off with the Moor simply to indulge a sophisticated but bored and rebellious young woman's taste for sexual novelty.

In fact, the conversation between Iago and Cassio revolves around Cassio's mistress Bianca. Not for the first time, Iago will use Cassio's public behaviour against him. Notice how Othello's thinking is now constructed almost entirely out of the material provided for him by Iago and how he misreads

Appearance and reality

every single element of Cassio's behaviour.

## 'How shall I murder him, Iago?'

Othello's only thought now is of how he should kill Cassio; he has no doubt

Desdemona

left in his mind as to the other's guilt. Othello also considers Desdemona's qualities, his speech and emotions swooping wildly between the extremes of a 'fine woman' who is 'delicate with her needle', and 'an admirable musician' and a woman who should 'rot, and perish, and be damned to-night'. In a gruesome echo of the kind of language we have come to associate most with Iago, Othello says he will 'chop her into messes'. Iago advises him instead to 'strangle her in her bed'.

## 'I have not deserv'd this.'

The arrival of Lodovico with a message from Venice distracts Othello for a

Othello

moment but, on hearing Desdemona express pleasure that Cassio may be made Governor because Othello is summoned back to Venice, he strikes her. Othello then proceeds to humiliate Desdemona in front of Lodovico as he sarcastically demonstrates how 'obedient' she is. This is the most unsympathetic side of Othello and reminds us again of the stereotype of the 'cruel Moor' which Iago attempted to pin on him at the start of the play. The rest of Othello's speech is a confused mixture of insults directed at Desdemona and matters contained in the letter from Venice.

Lodovico's comments about Othello's strange behaviour give Iago the

Iago

perfect opportunity to undermine his stature further by suggesting – in a reversal of his own self-description earlier in the play – that 'He's that he is'. Iago carefully avoids offering any description of what he thinks is wrong with Othello, being content to allow others to draw the 'obvious' conclusion for themselves.

When considering how much blame for the tragedy you might lay at Iago's door, bear in mind the evidence before Othello, a man of few social graces whose background is largely in the military world. Venetian women of the time did indeed have a reputation for sexual promiscuity and, whilst Desdemona is a wealthy woman from a family of social position, the relationship between Cassio and Bianca indicates the more common relationship between soldiers and women. Othello may be gullible – innocent, if you prefer – but there is no doubting the skill with which Iago manoeuvres his arguments, or the timing of his assaults.

# Act 4 Scene 2

*Othello closely questions Emilia. She defends Desdemona, who is then brought in. Othello ignores his wife's explanations, is clearly convinced of her guilt and storms out in a rage. Emilia and Iago try to reassure Desdemona about Othello's behaviour. Emilia realises that someone has poisoned Othello's mind, but Iago shrugs off this suggestion. Left alone, Iago meets an angry Roderigo, who wants to know what has happened to all the valuables he has given Iago as a reward for pleading his suit with Desdemona. Iago deflects Roderigo's threat to go and see Desdemona himself, and instead skillfully draws him into a plot to kill Cassio, so that Othello will have to stay and Desdemona will therefore remain in Cyprus also.*

### 'You have seen nothing, then?'

Othello questions Emilia, Desdemona's maid, in an attempt to verify his suspicions, but no matter how devoutly she swears that her mistress is honest his mind is made up. Othello assumes that if Emilia is telling the truth this must prove how devious and secretive Desdemona has been. His greeting to his wife: 'Pray, chuck, come hither' has an ominous and cold ring to it,

Othello

following his harsh treatment of her in the last scene.

### 'Had it pleas'd heaven
### To try me with affliction...'

Throughout this speech, as Othello explains his feelings to Desdemona, notice how he concentrates on himself: his honour, his position and his happiness. Some commentators see this as clear evidence that Iago was right to accuse Othello of arrogant selfishness and that he is in reality concerned only with himself. Others suggest that this speech is good evidence

Darkness
and light

of Othello's feelings of insecurity, his perception that as a Moor he is an outsider who is never really accepted into Venetian society and is therefore always acutely conscious of his own failings and isolation in the eyes of others. The imagery Othello uses about Desdemona contrasts vividly with that at the start of the play: his life, his soul has now become the dark pit or 'cistern' where 'foul toads' breed. This reinforces the animal imagery of Iago and the earlier echoes of creatures and places to do with black magic and witchcraft, and which were likened to Othello's pagan background.

### 'How have I been behav'd, that he might stick
### The smallest opinion, on my greatest abuse?'

Desdemona cannot understand why Othello is determined to turn everything she says against her. Othello has twisted the words she uses in just the way Iago does, emphasising the way his thinking now works along the same lines of that of his unrecognised enemy. Typically, when she summons Iago to

Desdemona

explain Othello's strange behaviour, he offers nothing.

### 'I will be hang'd, if some eternal villain...
### Have not devis'd this slander...'

Emilia

True to form, the perceptive Emilia hits upon the truth with a suddenness which seems to startle Iago, who declares that 'there is no such man, it is impossible'. Although he escapes unsuspected, this is a dangerous moment for Iago and one which heightens the dramatic tension, for the audience can see how close he comes to being discovered.

### 'O good Iago,
### What shall I do to win my lord again?'

In an echo of the earlier scene where Iago and Othello knelt to swear their

Angel and devil

common purpose in vengeance and hate, Desdemona here kneels to vow her love and loyalty to her husband. Both husband and wife have now knelt before Iago and put their future wellbeing into his stewardship. Desdemona's open and innocent feelings for Othello also contrast sharply with her husband's, emphasising that it is he who has suffered the greater fall in stature. Ironically, both Desdemona and Emilia here call for help to the one person who is most to blame for creating the situation.

### 'I do not find that thou deal'st justly with me.'

Although Roderigo finally seems to have realised that Iago has duped him,

Roderigo

he is easily persuaded that Iago is very close to obtaining the 'enjoyment' of Desdemona for him. Such is Roderigo's willingness to believe what Iago tells him that he will grasp at any chance that it may be true, however unsupported. In this respect, Roderigo's behaviour anticipates that of Othello, of whom he is a lesser echo. Iago is usually successful not because of the skill of his plots, but because of the weakness of his victims. Iago therefore easily persuades Roderigo that he must kill Cassio.

# Act 4 Scene 3

*Desdemona is sent to bed alone by Othello. In her room, she discusses her unhappiness with Emilia. Although she still loves Othello, Desdemona is depressed and morbid and sings a sad song from her youth about women who are abandoned in love. Emilia tries to reassure her with common-sense advice about the shortcomings of men.*

### 'Get you to bed on the instant'

It would be customary for a young woman of social position to have her maid sleep close to her mistress, usually in a nearby room or passage, but Othello orders her to be dismissed. Before they part for the night we see them discuss the events of the day in this short, sad scene.

### '... my love doth so approve him,
### That even his stubbornness, his checks and frowns...'

Love, jealousy, hatred

Desdemona's love for her husband is emphasised again, as is her innocent lack of understanding of the depth of Othello's feelings. However, we should note the ominous reference she makes to wanting Emilia to use her bed linen as her death shroud. This foreshadows the way Desdemona's bed will indeed shortly become her grave. Her song is a lament for a woman who finds sadness in love and her itching eyes 'bode weeping' for such a woman in ways she cannot know, but which the audience can anticipate.

### 'But I do think it is their husbands' faults
### If wives do fall...'

Emilia

In this conversation between Emilia and Desdemona we see highlighted the differences in character between them. Desdemona sees that love could never be compromised, whereas Emilia feels that she could succumb to lust – or even outright prostitution – if it served her purpose and that this would be acceptable if the reward were large enough. Emilia is at pains to point out that she would not be unfaithful for mere trinkets or small favours, nor would she wish her behaviour to become known, but that she considers herself reasonably moral. We might find Emilia the more recognisably human of the two women in this scene, confessing as she does that she is open to temptation, unlike Desdemona. But you should consider how you regard her view that it is acceptable to hurt in return someone who has hurt her. Does this strike you as a cynical, brutal and harsh view of the world, rather like her husband's, or do you instead feel that Desdemona is unrealistic and unconvincing in her devotion to fidelity and to certain standards of behaviour? Or are these two characters simply expressing a view of the workings of the world which reflects their different upbringing and social status? Whatever your conclusions, notice how they affect your view of the relationships between these two women and the other characters in the play.

# Self-test Questions Act Four

**Uncover the plot**

Delete two of the three alternatives given, to find the correct plot. Beware possible misconceptions and muddles.

Iago tells Othello that Cassio has denied/admitted/bragged about committing adultery with Desdemona. Othello faints/laughs/is silent. Othello agrees to arrange/spy on/attend a meeting between Iago and Cassio to talk about Desdemona. At the meeting Iago talks to Cassio about Bianca/Emilia/Cecilia. Bianca arrives, angry that the handkerchief belongs to another woman/is a copy/has gone missing. Othello thinks Cassio has given Desdemona's token of her love for him to a prostitute/his sister/another woman. Othello vows to divorce/beat/kill Desdemona. Lodovico/Montano/Brabantio arrives from Venice/Rhodes/Cyprus to say that Othello must return and that Cassio/Iago/Roderigo is to govern in his absence. Desdemona is pleased and Othello beats/kisses/embraces her. Iago says that Othello's behaviour these days is often loving/unkind/distracted. Othello closely questions Emilia/Bianca/Montano about his wife's behaviour. Othello accepts/is suspicious of/ignores his wife's explanations. Bianca/Cecilia/Emilia realises that someone has poisoned Othello's mind. Iago meets an angry Cassio/Gratiano/Roderigo who wants to know what has happened to all the valuables he has given him for pleading his suit with Desdemona. Iago skilfully draws him into a plot to kill Cassio/Othello/Desdemona. Desdemona is sent home/to bed/away alone by Othello; later she discusses her unhappiness with Emilia/Bianca/Cassio.

### Who? What? Why? When? Where? How?

1  Who in this act feels that he has not been justly dealt with by Iago?
2  Desdemona wonders whether itching eyes fortell what condition?
3  Which character feels that women would make their 'husband a cuckold, to make him a monarch'?
4  When Othello commands Desdemona to go to bed, what else does he also tell her to do?
5  Who accuses whom that his 'words and performances are no kin together'?
6  Iago tells Roderigo that Othello has been commanded to go to what country?
7  Of whom is it said that 'there's mettle in thee'?
8  In whose company does Othello strike his wife?
9  Whose idea is it for Othello to strangle Desdemona?
10  Who is the last character to speak to Desdemona in this act?

### Who said that?

1  'Stand you awhile apart,/Confine yourself but in a patient list.'
2  'How shall I murder him...?'
3  'I have not deserv'd this.'
4  'This is a subtle whore,/A closet, lock and key, of villainous secrets.'
5  'I will be hang'd, if some eternal villain,/Some busy and insinuating rogue...'
6  'Fie, there is no such man, it is impossible.'
7  'Lie with her, lie on her?'
8  'Was this fair paper, this most goodly book,/made to write "whore" on?'
9  'Do it not with poison...'
10  'Had it pleas'd heaven/To try me with affliction...'

### Open quotes

Identify the scene; complete the phrase; identify the speaker and the character being spoken to.

1  'Or to be naked with her friend abed,'
2  'The fountain, from which my current runs,/Or else dries up, to be discarded thence;'
3  'O thou black weed, why art so lovely fair?'
4  'Are not you a strumpet?'

5   '... even his stubbornness, his checks and frowns, –/Prithee unpin me, –'
6   'If that the earth could teem with women's tears,'
7   'But I do think it is their husbands' faults...'
8   'O good Iago,/What shall I do to win my lord again?'
9   'I cry you mercy,/I took you for that cunning whore of Venice,'
10  'I see that nose of yours...'

---

# Act 5 Scene 1

*On his way back from Bianca's house at night, Cassio is attacked by Roderigo, whom he wounds. Cassio is wounded by Iago, who escapes unseen, disappointed in his hopes that the two men would kill each other. Othello arrives and assumes that Iago has attacked Cassio. Brabantio's relatives Lodovico and Gratiano arrive and meet the returning Iago; whilst they help Cassio, Iago secretly kills Roderigo. As the injured Cassio is carried off, Iago begins to hint that he and Roderigo fought over Bianca, with whom Cassio has spent some time that night. When Emilia learns of this she rounds on Bianca and accuses her of being a common prostitute.*

## "Tis but a man gone: forth, my sword, he dies.'

This scene echoes that at the start of the play, where Iago and Roderigo met

Darkness and light

at night to plot their earlier intrigue and treachery. It is in the same way symbolic of the way the action is driven by the darker reaches of the soul. Ironically, Roderigo's words here, as he strikes at Cassio, foreshadow his own death and the casual way in which Iago dismisses it as being of little consequence. The excuse comes a few lines further on, when Iago pretends to happen upon the wounded Cassio and, in helping him, stabs and kills the wounded Roderigo. Notice the subtle irony at this later point, for only the treacherous and black-hearted Iago has a light.

## 'Iago! O, I am spoil'd, undone by villains!
## Give me some help.'

With dramatic irony Cassio calls out to Iago, of all characters, to help save him

Iago

from the villains who have sought to undo him. Iago had hoped that Cassio and Roderigo would kill each other so that he might be rid of both of them, but takes advantage of the darkness to murder the wounded Roderigo in cold blood. Notice how even at this stage the references to 'honest' Iago abound, and the irony with which Iago calls Cassio's attackers 'treacherous villains'.

Shakespeare uses the rapid action of this scene, with characters continually coming and going, and with short and broken lines of speech, to emphasise the confusion within the minds of characters. Significantly, it is Othello's mistake in thinking that Iago has killed Cassio that spurs him on to murder Desdemona. Like his other mistaken perceptions, this one will also lead Othello into further self-destruction.

**'This is the night**
**That either makes me, or fordoes me quite.'**
Iago's aside here emphasises for the audience the critical importance of the next part of the play, upon which everything hangs, and this increases the tension as we move into the final scene.

# Act 5 Scene 2

*At the bedside of the sleeping Desdemona, Othello determines to kill her, but not to destroy her beauty. As she wakens, he tells her to prepare for death, giving the evidence of the handkerchief as proof of her guilt. Desdemona says that Cassio will vouchsafe her innocence, but Othello says he is already dead and smothers her. Emilia has been knocking at the door and when Othello admits her she tells him that Cassio is alive but Roderigo is dead. Desdemona recovers enough to declare her innocence just before she dies. Othello tells Emilia that he has killed Desdemona because of the adultery which Iago has told him about. Emilia now knows who has poisoned Othello's mind and calls for help. Montano, Gratiano and Iago come in and Emilia reveals how she gave the handkerchief to Iago. Othello realises what has happened and attacks Iago, who stabs Emilia and escapes. Emilia dies as Montano and Gratiano search for Iago. Lodovico, Montano and the wounded Cassio enter with the captured Iago, whom Othello again attacks and this time wounds. In response to Othello's demands to know why he behaved as he did, Iago refuses to speak. Cassio supports Desdemona's innocence and Othello, distraught at his own foolishness, kills himself.*

**'Put out the light, and then put out the light...'**
In a significant dramatic echo, we see Othello enter from the darkness with

**Darkness and light**

a light, just as did Iago in the last scene. The connection between these two characters is that the will of one has come to rule the heart of the other. There is also a dramatic irony in Othello, whose actions have been overwhelmed by the evil of Iago, bringing illumination into the darkness. Like Iago, Othello has come to destroy goodness, although he actually sees himself as Desdemona's redeemer. Othello says of the light that he carries that he 'can again thy former light restore' if he should choose, but that if he kills the sleeping Desdemona he cannot make her 'light relume'. He understands the enormity of the action which he is contemplating, but cannot rid himself of the emotional turmoil inside him which he knows is driving him to act. This complex play of the imagery of light and dark as symbols of goodness, the spirit and evil therefore echoes the way the darkness of Othello's soul and the blackness of his skin are used to represent his inner confusion and, earlier in the play, were used to emphasise his outer grace. The whiteness of Desdemona's skin here symbolises her inner purity and

Love, jealousy, hatred

innocence, which Othello, ironically, says he cannot bear to mark. Notice also the use of other opposites in the language, as when Othello says that Desdemona's sweetness has been 'fatal', that he weeps 'cruel tears' because his murderous act is 'heavenly' – 'it strikes where it does love' and he is both cruel and merciful in what he is doing. See the section on themes and images at the start of this guide for more background on these ideas.

Othello sees his killing of Desdemona as 'justice' for her foul deeds. He

Othello

is angry when she denies any wrongdoing because it 'makest me call what I intend to do/A murder, which I thought a sacrifice'. There is a strong mixture in the scene of the public figure of Othello, doing his duty, and the intensely personal emotions of the man: Desdemona's skin is 'smooth, as monumental alabaster', she is 'rose', and her 'balmy breath' almost persuades him to abandon his act. Although Othello characterises his deed as 'justice' it is significant that, unlike the Duke of Venice, he will hear only one side of the story. He rejects Desdemona's pleas to call Cassio and ask him whether she speaks the truth in the mistaken belief that he has been killed. This is yet another dramatic and ironic moment in the play, where a golden opportunity to explode Iago's lies and avert the tragedy is missed.

## 'Good gentlemen, let me have leave to speak, 'Tis proper I obey him, but not now…'

Emilia insists on being allowed to speak, in spite of her husband's attempts

Emilia

to quieten her. By her actions here Emilia reveals that she is an honest character not without moral standards, as we also saw when she rounded on Bianca and accused her of being a common prostitute in Act 5, scene 1. She realises that Iago has until now relied upon her unthinking obedience as a shield and out of a sense of shock and horror, she vigorously exposes his lies. Notice how, after Iago has stabbed her and she lies dying, the parallels between Emilia and Desdemona are echoed when she sings part of the willow song which her mistress sang in Act 4, scene 3. Both women have been forsaken and killed by their husbands. Emilia's faith in Desdemona is unquestioning to the last, her reaction to the news of Othello's suspicion being that he is foolish to think so. Emilia seems to have had the kind of implicit trust in Desdemona's purity which we might have expected from

Othello, hinting that – unlike Othello – her robust and worldly-wise attitude may have made her immune to the kind of character assassination which Iago practised on Othello.

### 'O look down towards his feet, but that's a fable –
### If that thou be'st a devil, I cannot kill thee.'

Othello emphasises the idea, which runs through the play, that Iago is the

personification of the devil himself. Although Othello wounds Iago with his sword, it is dramatically significant that he does not in fact kill him, as Iago gloatingly points out: 'I bleed, sir, but not killed' are almost the last words he speaks. Whilst Othello may have been an outsider because of his military

**Angel and devil**   background, his culture and the colour of his skin, we see at the end of the play that Iago is now isolated; he is morally and spiritually excluded from society. Iago's evil is emphasised at the end of the play and this strengthens the audience's sense of relief that such a creature has been caught and will now be tortured. But what is important is not just that an evil troublemaker has been caught, for what Iago has destroyed in Othello and Desdemona is the potential for harmony and goodness in the world. Although *Othello* has been called a domestic tragedy, it addresses itself just as much to the universal themes of order and disorder as do those of Shakespeare's plays which have a more easily identified cosmic sweep to their action.

### 'An honourable murderer, if you will:
### For nought did I in hate, but all in honour.'

How far can we feel sympathy for Othello at this moment, and how far can we agree with him? Like Hamlet and King Lear, Othello realises too late that his fate is to become the instrument of his own destruction.

### 'I kiss'd thee ere I kill'd thee – no way but this,
### Killing myself, to die upon a kiss.'

Why does Othello take his own life? You may feel that his suicide is the only

courageous soldierly option open to him, or you may think that in his despair he escapes into death because his spirit is broken. It is perhaps a contradictory mixture of both which we witness here, reinforcing again the play's central theme of the ambiguity which exists between appearance and reality and underlining the impossibility of ever knowing for certain

**Othello**   the real motives of others, and perhaps of ourselves. In his death Othello seems to regain some of his earlier nobility in a way which echoes Macbeth – both men regain a clearer and saner perspective on the world only when it is too late. Othello dies declaring his love for Desdemona with a kiss.

Angel and devil

The play's theme was a popular one in the Medieval Morality Plays which were well known at the time. Such plays took as a common theme the way a noble and highly regarded person may fall to the depths of depravity, often through a single error of judgement or weakness of character, but that within them will exist a troubled soul which will eventually bring them to accept their fate. In the Morality plays the central character was set between an angel and a devil and made to choose between them. The entertainment in such plays derived from the main character's temptation into sin and their eventual return to the angel's forgiveness.

'O Spartan dog,
More fell than anguish, hunger or the sea!
Look on the tragic lodging of this bed:
This is thy work...'

Appearance and reality

As Lodovico speaks the closing lines of the play, the central notion of the gulf which may exist between appearance and reality surfaces for the final time. Iago's evil plotting has so corrupted the marriage of Othello and Desdemona that the sight of their two bodies, united again in death, poisons the eye of the beholder just as Iago's lies poisoned Othello's thoughts.

# Self-test Questions Act Five

### Uncover the plot
Delete two of the three alternatives given, to find the correct plot. Beware possible misconceptions and muddles.

On his way back from the house of Desdemona/Emilia/Bianca at night, Cassio/Montano/Othello is attacked by Lodovico/Roderigo/Brabantio, whom he wounds. Cassio/Montano/Othello is then wounded by Roderigo/Othello/Iago. Iago secretly kills Roderigo/Montano/Brabantio. Iago hints that the fight was over Emilia/Cecilia/Bianca. Othello says he will kill the sleeping Desdemona but not cause her pain/destroy her beauty/waken her. He says the handkerchief/her confession/Cassio's death is proof of her guilt and strangles/smothers/stabs her. Othello eventually realises what has happened and attacks Iago, who blames/ stabs/hits Emilia, who dies/faints/escapes. The wounded Cassio/Roderigo/Lodovico enters with the captured Iago. Iago refuses to speak/confess/return to Venice. Montano/Emilia/Cassio supports Desdemona's innocence and Othello is taken away/is stabbed/kills himself.

### Who? What? Why? When? Where? How?
1 Who says he thought Othello had no weapon?
2 Who tells Othello that 'your power and your command is taken off'?

3    What is Desdemona's final request to Othello?
4    Which two characters are plotting together as this act opens?
5    What are Desdemona's last words?
6    Of what did Brabantio die?
7    Who is crying out to be let in as Othello kills Desdemona?
8    Who kills Emilia and how?
9    Who has 'a daily beauty in his life'?
10   Who kills Roderigo?

## Who said that?

1    'I do suspect this trash/To bear a part in this…'
2    ' 'Tis proper I obey him, but not now.'
3    '… the object poisons sight.'
4    'Fie,/your sword upon a woman?'
5    'Be near at hand, I may miscarry in't.'
6    'Thou hast not half the power to do me harm/As I have to be hurt.'
7    'Have you prayed to-night, Desdemona?'
8    'What should such a fool/Do with so good a woman?'
9    'Yet she must die, else she'll betray more men.'
10   'Tis but a man gone: forth, my sword, he dies.'

## Open quotes

Identify the scene; complete the phrase; identify the speaker and the character being spoken to.

1    'I am no strumpet, …'
2    'O, the more angel she,'
3    '… look down towards his feet, but that's a fable,'
4    'I kiss'd thee ere I kille'd thee, no way but this…'
5    'Put out the light …'
6    'An honourable murderer, if you will…'
7    '… yet I'll not shed her blood,/Nor scar that whiter …'
8    'This look of thine will hurl my soul from heaven,'
9    '… then must you speak/Of one that lov'd not wisely,'
10   'Blow me about in winds, roast me in sulphur,'

# Self-test Answers Act One

**Uncover the plot**

Roderigo loves Desdemona and has been paying Iago to help him court her. Iago confesses that he hates his master. Desdemona's father, Brabantio, does not know about her elopement and is woken and told about it. Othello is warned by Iago about his anger. Desdemona's father accuses Othello of using witchcraft to seduce his daughter. The Turkish fleets appear to be sailing towards the Venetian territory of Cyprus, which it seems they may invade. Desdemona's father makes his complaint about his daughter's marriage and Othello responds. Desdemona is sent for to give her side of the story and supports Othello's defence that they are in love. Her father accepts this, reluctantly. Desdemona is allowed to travel after her husband, accompanied by Iago. Iago says that Desdemona will soon regret her marriage to a Moor. Iago comments on how easily he extracts money from the foolish Roderigo and how he plans to revenge himself upon Othello and Cassio by making his master believe that the latter is Desdemona's lover.

**Who? What? Why? When? Where? How?**

1   Iago says this to Brabantio when the latter is reluctant to believe the news about Desdemona's elopement because he thinks that Iago and Roderigo are ruffians
2   Brabantio's description of his daughter seems in error because she appears soon after this to defend her husband boldly and declare her love for him
3   The Anthropophagi, and men whose; heads/Do grow beneath their shoulders
4   A hundred and seven; then two hundred; then thirty
5   Iago says this of Cassio
6   Iago tells Othello that he thought to kill Brabantio because of his insults about Othello's honour
7   Brabantio says this about his daughter's elopement
8   Iago says this to Roderigo
9   Iago says this of Othello and, because it is spoken in a soliloquy, we may assume it to be a true reflection of Iago's mind. This shows us Iago's keen observation of the human weakness in Othello, which he will use to destroy him
10   Iago says this to Brabantio as a lewd description of Othello and Desdemona's love-making

**Who said that?**

1   Roderigo (1,1)
2   Othello (1,2)
3   The Duke, talking about Brabantio's accusations that Othello used witchcraft or drugs to win his daughter (1,2)
4   Desdemona, answering her father's question as to whom she owes most obedience (1,3)
5   Iago, talking to Roderigo (1,3)
6   The Duke (1,3)
7   Othello (1,3)
8   Iago, talking to Brabantio (1,1)
9   Brabantio, talking to Iago (1,1)
10   Iago (1,1)

1  'For doves to peck at: I am not what I am.' Iago, talking to Roderigo (1,1)
2  'Shall manifest me rightly.' Othello, talking to Iago (1,2)
3  'Your son-in-law is far more fair than black.' The Duke, talking to Brabantio about Othello (1,3)
4  'He's done my office.' Iago, speaking in his soliloquy (1,3), of his suspicions about Othello
5  'He comes to bad intent.' Iago, speaking to Othello (1,2)
6  'And I lov'd her that she did pity them.' Othello, talking (1,3) to the Duke and his court about how he and Desdemona came to love each other
7  'We cannot all be masters, nor all masters/Cannot be truly follow'd.' Iago, speaking to Roderigo about Othello (1,1)
8  'for the dew will rust 'em.' Othello, talking to Iago, Brabantio and followers (1,2)
9  'She has deceiv'd her father, and may thee.' Brabantio, speaking to Othello about Desdemona (1,3)
10  'And little blest with the soft phrase of peace.' Othello, speaking to the Duke and his court in (1,2)

# Self-test Answers Act Two

**Uncover the plot**

The action of the play has now moved to Cyprus. News arrives that the Turkish fleet has been scattered. Iago tells Roderigo that Desdemona really loves Cassio but says that she will love him soon. Roderigo is persuaded to pick a fight with Cassio whilst he is on duty and thus disgrace him. Iago seems determined to believe that Othello has committed adultery with Emilia. A great celebration is held to honour the consummation of Othello's marriage. Iago gets Cassio drunk and argumentative. Cassio argues and fights with Roderigo. Iago tells Montano that Cassio is prone to drunkenness and fighting. As he tries to separate a quarrel, Montano is wounded. Cassio is dismissed from his position by Othello. Iago encourages him to seek Desdemona's help in persuading Othello to change his mind. Left alone, Iago says he will get Othello to misinterpret this.

**Who? What? Why? When? Where? How?**
1  Cassio tells Desdemona this when talking about Iago (2,1)
2  Iago
3  Roderigo
4  Cassio
5  Montano
6  Roderigo complains to Iago about this
7  Desdemona's, according to Iago
8  Desdemona, according to Iago
9  Cassio, although he is drunk at the time
10  Iago describes Roderigo in this way

**Who said that?**
1  Iago (2,1)
2  Iago, talking about Cassio (2,1)
3  Othello, talking to Montano and others about their fighting (2,3)

4   Roderigo (2,3)
5   Iago (2,3)
6   Desdemona (2,1)
7   Montano, speaking of Othello (2,1)
8   Iago (2,1)
9   Othello (2,3)
10  Cassio (2,3)

### Open quotes

1   'As of her tongue she has bestow'd on me,/You'd have enough.' Iago, talking about Emilia to Cassio (2,1)
2   'May the winds blow, till they have waken'd death.' Othello, talking to Desdemona upon his arrival in Cyprus (2,1)
3   '... oft got without merit, and lost without deserving.' Iago, talking to Cassio (2,3)
4   'Saints in your injuries; devils being offended;/Players in your housewifery; and housewives in your beds.' Iago, speaking to Emilia and Desdemona (2,1)
5   'I'll set down the pegs that make this music,/As honest as I am.' Iago, in an aside in (2,1)
6   '...well enough, and speak well enough.' Cassio, speaking to the revellers (2,3)
7   'Cassio, I love thee,/But never more be officer of mine.' Othello, talking to Iago and Cassio (2,3)
8   'I ha' lost my reputation!' Cassio, talking to Iago (2,3)
9   'They do suggest at first with heavenly shows.' Iago, in a soliloquy (2,3)
10  'But does foul pranks, which fair and wise ones do.' Iago, talking to Desdemona (2,1)

# Self-test Answers Act Three

### Uncover the plot

Cassio has arranged for some musicians to serenade Othello and Desdemona the morning after their nuptial celebrations. Iago arrives and says he will get Emilia to see Cassio at once and will also distract Othello so that they may speak freely. Desdemona has already begun to plead for Cassio. Desdemona pleads with Othello on Cassio's behalf. Iago skilfully steers Othello's feelings towards jealousy about Cassio's relationships with Desdemona. Emilia picks up a handkerchief – Othello's first present to Desdemona – which she has unknowingly dropped. She gives the handkerchief to Iago. Iago tells Othello that Cassio has talked in his sleep about his love for Desdemona and that Iago has seen him wiping his beard with her handkerchief. Othello asks Desdemona for the handkerchief, saying it has special magical powers. Desdemona says it is not lost. Othello becomes furious. Cassio is visited by Bianca, his mistress, who gently scolds him for not visiting her more often. Cassio asks her to copy a handkerchief he has found.

### Who? What? Why? When? Where? How?

1   The handkerchief which Othello gave Desdemona
2   Iago
3   Cassio

4   Iago says he will put it there for him to find
5   Cassio and Bianca
6   Othello and Iago (3,3)
7   An Egyptian charmer
8   Because, according to the clown, Othello does not like the noise they are making
9   He had a toothache
10  Emilia, who finds it where it has been dropped by Desdemona on the floor by accident

### Who said that?
1   Iago, of Cassio (3,3)
2   Iago (3,3)
3   Emilia (3,3)
4   Othello (3,3)
5   Othello, to Desdemona (3,3)
6   Emilia (3,3)
7   Cassio (3,4)
8   Cassio (3,4)
9   Iago (3,3)
10  Othello, to Desdemona, who has just left (3,3)

### Open quotes
1   'All my abilities in thy behalf.' Desdemona, talking to Cassio (3,3)
2   'That chamberers have, or for I am declin'd/Into the vale of years.' Othello, in a soliloquy (3,3)
3   'Confirmations strong/As proofs of holy writ.' Iago, in a soliloquy (3,3)
4   'Drew all such humours from him.' Desdemona, talking to Emilia about Othello (3,4)
5   'And she speaks for you stoutly.' Emilia, talking to Cassio (3,1)
6   'I think that thou are just, and think thou art not.' Othello, talking to Iago (3,3)
7   'Sometimes intrude not?' Iago, talking to Othello (3,3)
8   'And we all but food.' Emilia, talking to Desdemona about men (3,4)
9   'And live upon the vapour in a dungeon,/Than keep a corner in a thing I love,/For others' uses.' Othello, in a soliloquy (3,3)
10  'the green-ey'd monster, which doth mock/That meat it feeds on.' Iago, talking to Othello (3,3)

# Self-test Answers Act Four

### Uncover the plot
Iago tells Othello that Cassio has admitted committing adultery with Desdemona. Othello faints. Othello agrees to spy on a meeting between Iago and Cassio to talk about Desdemona. At the meeting Iago talks to Cassio about Bianca. Bianca arrives, angry that the handkerchief belongs to another woman. Othello thinks Cassio has given Desdemona's token of her love for him to a prostitute. Othello vows to kill Desdemona. Lodovico arrives from Venice to say that Othello must return and that Cassio is to govern in his absence. Desdemona is pleased and Othello beats her. Iago says that Othello's behaviour these days is often unkind.

Othello closely questions Emilia about his wife's behaviour. Othello ignores his wife's explanations. Emilia realises that someone has poisoned Othello's mind. Iago meets an angry Roderigo who wants to know what has happened to all the valuables he has given him for pleading his suit with Desdemona. Iago skilfully draws him into a plot to kill Cassio. Desdemona is sent to bed alone by Othello; later she discusses her unhappiness with Emilia.

## Who? What? Why? When? Where? How?
1 Roderigo
2 Weeping
3 Emilia tells Desdemona that she and most other women would do this
4 To dismiss Emilia from her room
5 Roderigo accuses Iago of this
6 Mauritania
7 Roderigo, according to Iago
8 Lodovico's and Iago's
9 Iago's
10 Emilia

## Who said that?
1 Iago, to Othello (4,1)
2 Othello (4,1)
3 Desdemona (4,1)
4 Othello (4,2)
5 Emilia (4,2)
6 Iago (4,2)
7 Othello (4,1)
8 Othello (4,2)
9 Iago (4,1)
10 Othello (4,2)

## Open quotes
1 'An hour, or more, not meaning any harm?' Iago, talking to Othello (4,1)
2 'Or keep it as a cistern, for foul toads/To knot and gender in!' Othello, talking to Desdemona (4,2)
3 'Thou smell'st so sweet, that the sens aches at thee,/Would thou hadst ne'er been born!' Othello, talking to Desdemona (4,2)
4 'No, as I am a Christian.' Desdemona, answering the question from Othello (4,2)
5 '… have grace and favour in them.' Desdemona, talking to Emilia (4,3)
6 'Each drop she falls would prove a crocodile.' Othello, talking about Desdemona (in her presence) to Lodovico (4,1)
7 'If wives do fall.' Emilia, talking to Desdemona about men (4,3)
8 'Good friend, go to him, for, by this light of heaven,/I know not how I lost him.' Desdemona (4,2)
9 'That married with Othello.' Othello, talking to Desdemona (4,2)
10 '… but not that dog I shall throw't to.' Othello, about Cassio, whilst overhearing the latter's conversation with Iago, therefore effectively in a soliloquy (4,1)

# Self-test Answers Act Five

### Uncover the plot
On his way back from the house of Bianca at night, Cassio is attacked by Roderigo, whom he wounds. Cassio is then wounded by Iago. Iago secretly kills Roderigo. Iago hints that the fight was over Bianca. Othello says he will kill the sleeping Desdemona but not destroy her beauty. He says the handkerchief is proof of her guilt and smothers her. Othello eventually realises what has happened and attacks Iago, who stabs Emilia, who dies. The wounded Cassio enters with the captured Iago. Iago refuses to speak. Cassio supports Desdemona's innocence and Othello kills himself.

### Who? What? Why? When? Where? How?
1 Cassio
2 Lodovico
3 That he allow her 'But a half an hour, but while I say one prayer!'
4 Iago and Roderigo
5 Commend me to my kind lord, O, farewell!
6 Grief
7 Emilia
8 Iago, by stabbing her
9 Cassio
10 Iago

### Who said that?
1 Iago, of Bianca (5,1)
2 Emilia (5,2)
3 Lodovico (5,2)
4 Gratiano (5,2)
5 Roderigo (5,1)
6 Emilia (5,2)
7 Othello (5,2)
8 Emilia (5,2)
9 Othello, of Desdemona (5,2)
10 Roderigo (5,1)

### Open quotes
1 '...but of life as honest/As you, that thus abuse me.' Bianca, talking to Emilia (5,1)
2 'And you the blacker devil.' Emilia, talking to Othello (5,2)
3 'If that thou be'st a devil, I cannot kill thee.' Othello, talking to Iago (5,2)
4 'Killing myself, to die upon a kiss.' Othello, talking to the dead Desdemona (5,2)
5 '... and then put out the light.' Othello, speaking over the sleeping Desdemona (5,2)
6 'For nought did I in hate, but all in honour.' Othello, talking to Lodovico, Montano and Cassio (5,2)
7 'skin of hers than snow,/And smooth, as monumental alabaster.' Othello, speaking over the sleeping Desdemona (5,2)
8 'And fiends will snatch at it.' Othello, talking to Gratiano (5,2)
9 'but too well.' Othello, talking to Lodovico (5,2)
10 'Wash me in steep-down gulfs of liquid fire!' Othello, talking to Gratiano and Emilia (5,2)